Tours
etc

510 - 981 -
9844

ALSO BY JIMMY CARTER

Christmas in Plains: Memories (illustrated by Amy Carter)

An Hour Before Daylight: Memories of a Rural Boyhood

The Virtues of Aging

Sources of Strength: Meditations on Scripture for a Living Faith

Living Faith

The Little Baby Snoogle-Fleejer (illustrated by Amy Carter)

Always a Reckoning and Other Poems

Talking Peace: A Vision for the Next Generation

Turning Point: A Candidate, a State, and a Nation Come of Age

An Outdoor Journal: Adventures and Reflections

*Everything to Gain: Making the Most of the Rest of
Your Life* (with Rosalynn Carter)

The Blood of Abraham: Insights into the Middle East

Negotiation: The Alternative to Hostility

Keeping Faith: Memoirs of a President

A Government as Good as Its People

Why Not the Best?

FAITH

A Journey for All

JIMMY CARTER

Simon & Schuster Paperbacks

NEW YORK   LONDON   TORONTO
SYDNEY   NEW DELHI

Simon & Schuster
An Imprint of Simon & Schuster, Inc.
1230 Avenue of the Americas
New York, NY 10020

First Simon & Schuster trade paperback edition April 2019

SIMON & SCHUSTER PAPERBACKS and colophon are
registered trademarks of Simon & Schuster, Inc.

For information about special discounts for bulk purchases, please contact
Simon & Schuster Special Sales at 1-866-506-1949 or business@simonandschuster.com.

The Simon & Schuster Speakers Bureau can bring authors to your
live event. For more information or to book an event, contact
the Simon & Schuster Speakers Bureau at 1-866-248-3049
or visit our website at www.simonspeakers.com.

Interior design by Paul Dippolito

Manufactured in the United States of America

1   3   5   7   9   10   8   6   4   2

The Library of Congress has cataloged the hardcover edition as follows:

Names: Carter, Jimmy, 1924– author.
Title: Faith : a journey for all / Jimmy Carter.
Description: First Simon & Schuster hardcover edition. | New York : Simon
    & Schuster, 2018. | Includes index.
Identifiers: LCCN 2018003986 (print) | LCCN 2018005243 (ebook) | ISBN
    9781501184420 | ISBN 9781501184413 (hardcover : alk. paper) | ISBN
    9781501184437 (trade pbk. : alk. paper)
Subjects: LCSH: Faith. | Christianity and culture. | History—Religious
    aspects—Christianity.
Classification: LCC BV4637 (ebook) | LCC BV4637 .C346 2018
    (print) | DDC 234/.23—dc23
LC record available at https://lccn.loc.gov/2018003986

ISBN 978-1-5011-8441-3
ISBN 978-1-5011-8443-7 (pbk)
ISBN 978-1-5011-8442-0 (ebook)

This book is dedicated to my wife, Rosalynn,
who has shared all kinds of faith with me
for more than seventy years.

CONTENTS

AUTHOR'S NOTE

These are some people of faith whose works I reviewed before writing this book. I do not claim to understand all their theological or philosophical premises, but over the years I have jotted down and retained excerpts from their voluminous works with which I agree. Their quotes in this book will help us understand their basic beliefs.

My admiration for Reinhold Niebuhr (1892–1971) is well known. I quoted him in 1975, in *Why Not the Best?,* my first book. He was an unusual theologian, who, through his writings, exerted a great influence on American public affairs. He certainly had a powerful effect on my attitudes toward politics.

Reinhold's brother H. Richard Niebuhr (1894–1962) engaged less in public affairs, but he also was a distinguished American theologian and ethicist. His book, *Faith on Earth: An Inquiry into the Structure of Human Faith,* was given to me by his son, Richard, when it was published posthumously in 1989. It was especially helpful for this book.

Two American Christian thinkers and activists, whom I knew personally, were William Sloane Coffin (1924–2006) and

AUTHOR'S NOTE

Clarence Jordan (1912–1969). Both were controversial. Coffin had supported the civil rights movement, but he became best known as a leader of the peace movement during the Vietnam War. He served as chaplain at Yale, and later became senior minister at Riverside Church in New York, where he invited me to speak. He wrote a popular book, *The Heart Is a Little to the Left: Essays on Public Morality.*

Clarence Jordan was a fellow Georgian. In fact, his nephew, Hamilton Jordan, was one of my closest aides and became my White House chief of staff. Clarence Jordan was a New Testament Greek scholar who translated New Testament books into "Cotton Patch" versions, using Southern colloquial language. His book of Matthew was adapted into *The Cotton Patch Gospel,* an off-Broadway musical. A collection of his sermons has been published as *The Substance of Faith: And Other Cotton Patch Sermons.* I contributed the foreword. In 1942, Jordan founded Koinonia, a racially integrated religious community in southwest Georgia near Plains. As the civil rights movement advanced in the 1950s, Koinonia was perceived as a threat and suffered boycotts and violence. To me, Jordan was a model of courage and faith.

I studied two influential Swiss theologians, Karl Barth (1886–1968) and Emil Brunner (1889–1966). Barth often has been described as the most important theologian of the twentieth century. As a professor at German universities, he opposed Hitler and the Nazis. Of all the theologians I have read, Barth has been the most difficult for me to understand. His discussions of election, or predestination, have been enlightening if I understand his writings: that Jesus was predestined to be born as divine, but that God does not decide in advance which persons are destined to be saved or condemned. Brunner also has had an international impact. He respected but disagreed with certain teachings of Barth. I was especially interested in his discussion of the divine aspects of Jesus' life.

Three German theologians whom I read were Dietrich Bonhoeffer (1906–1945), Rudolf Karl Bultmann (1884–1976), and Jürgen Moltmann (b. 1926). Like Barth, Bonhoeffer was a theologian and founding member of the German Confessing Church, which opposed the Nazis. However, he remained in Germany during the war, was arrested, and executed. The knowledge of Bonhoeffer's personal courage has made me feel inadequate in my Christian life but has been inspirational in its impact.

Bultmann also supported the Confessing Church, but he did not directly oppose the Nazis. As a scholar, he critically analyzed the Gospel writings. He came to the conclusion that Christian faith is not about the historical Jesus, but about the transcendent Christ. What is important to faith is the resurrection and the proclamation of the New Testament. The explanations of Bultmann about the truly significant aspects of Christ have been helpful to me in dealing with arguments about the historical Jesus.

I had the opportunity to meet Jürgen Moltmann at Emory University, where I have been University Distinguished Professor since 1982, and Moltmann was a Distinguished Visiting Professor of Systematic Theology from 1983 to 1993. He is known for his theology of hope. He believes that God suffers through humanity, while also promising humanity a better future through the hope of the resurrection. This premise strengthens my own belief that God has eventual plans for a world of peace and harmony.

Søren Kierkegaard (1813–1855) was a Danish philosopher and theologian who is considered a major influence on existentialism and modern Protestant theology. He was a critic of organized religion, particularly the Church of Denmark. His emphasis is on one's personal relationship with God, which comes through faith. Much of his work deals with Christian love, and I quote him quite frequently in my Bible classes.

The final two thinkers I want to mention might not seem to fit the description of people of faith. Both Immanuel Kant (1774–1804) and Stephen Jay Gould (1941–2002) rejected traditional religion. Kant, a German philosopher, helped to shape almost every philosophical movement that followed him. I was especially interested in his explanation of the relationship between a person's ability to think and to reason and then to decide that an ethical and moral life is best. Gould, an American paleontologist and Harvard University professor, became known for popular writing about science. He especially focused on evolutionary theory, which reflected his scholarly work as well. Many of his books are in my library. I questioned him on some of his writings, and he usually responded to my criticisms in his next book. His writings helped to convince me that there cannot be any conflicts between scientific knowledge and religious beliefs.

In this book, I quote extensively from the Bible, particularly from the New Testament. Although I published *The NIV Lessons from Life Bible: Personal Reflections with Jimmy Carter,* and think well of it, I did not limit myself to the NIV translation for this book. During my life, I have used many translations, beginning with the King James Version. The theologians I consulted also used a variety of translations. The quotes in the book reflect notes I have taken over many years.

Some of the books in my library that I have consulted in writing this text:

Courage to Change: An Introduction to the Life and Thought of Reinhold Niebuhr—June Bingham
Ethics—Dietrich Bonhoeffer
Kierkegaard, Heidegger, Buber and Barth: Subject and Object in Modern Theology—James Brown
The Philosophy of Schopenhauer—Irwin Edman
Rocks of Ages: Science and Religion in the Fullness of Life— Stephen Jay Gould
A Layman's Guide to Protestant Theology—William Hordern
The Substance of Faith: And Other Cotton Patch Sermons— Clarence Jordan
The Primacy of Faith—Richard Kroner
On Being a Christian—Hans Küng

Human Destiny—Pierre Lecomte du Noüy

On Human Dignity: Political Theology and Ethics—Jürgen
    Moltmann

Theology of Hope—Jürgen Moltmann

Justice & Mercy—Reinhold Niebuhr

Faith on Earth: An Inquiry into the Structure of Human Faith—
    H. Richard Niebuhr (edited by Richard R. Niebuhr)

Reinhold Niebuhr on Politics: His Political Philosophy and Its
    Application to Our Age as Expressed in His Writings—
    (edited by Harry R. Davis and Robert C. Good)

Foundations of Christian Faith: An Introduction to the Idea of
    Christianity—Karl Rahner

An Altar in the World: A Geography of Faith—Barbara Brown
    Taylor

Building the Earth—Pierre Teilhard de Chardin

The Eternal Now—Paul Tillich

INTRODUCTION

Living faith always involves love. —Richard Niebuhr

Faith without works is not faith at all, but a simple lack of obedience to God. —Dietrich Bonhoeffer

The only thing that counts is faith expressing itself through love. —Galatians 5:6

The issue of faith arises in almost every area of human existence, so it is important to understand its multiple meanings. For many of us, a question that needs to be answered is "Am I a person of faith?" The answer is almost always affirmative. In this book, my primary goal is to explore the broader meaning of faith, its far-reaching effect on our lives, and its relationship to past, present, and future events in America and around the world. I also emphasize the religious aspects of faith since this is how the word is most often used, and I have included a description of the ways my own faith has guided and sustained me, as well as how it has challenged and driven me to seek a closer and better relationship with people and with God. Faith, in both its religious and broader dimensions, influences our individual and communal lives, our lives in religion, and our lives in government and in secular affairs.

The most important element of faith ever imposed on me, and on another person simultaneously, involved the threat of the total elimination of human life on earth by a nuclear war with the Soviet Union. My ultimate responsibility as President of the United States was to defend my country against a military attack, and I learned soon after my election that we and the Soviets had enough atomic weapons in our arsenals to destroy each other and that the resulting radiation and other collateral damage would kill most of the rest of the world's population. This was a constant haunting realization that dominated my conscious hours during my term in office—and I shared the responsibility with Leonid Brezhnev, President of the Soviet Union. Our common goal, of course, was to avoid a nuclear war. Brezhnev and I had to have faith in ourselves, and in each other. Every decision I made was affected by this threat, and *it still exists,* as the same responsibility is passed on from one president to the next.

We face many issues within which religion, politics, and private matters tend to mix, sometimes explosively, creating sharp divisions among us, in our private and public lives and between and within religious denominations. It is increasingly difficult to keep issues of religion and government separate, as even the purely religious issues are routinely addressed by politicians—and vice versa. I have confronted the separation of government and religion from both directions. I think often of the strong reaction of our visiting revival preacher in my mother's home when I decided to run for the state senate back in 1962. He asked me, "How can you, as a Christian, a deacon, and a Sunday School teacher, become involved in the dirty business of politics?" Without thinking, I gave him a smart-aleck response: "I will have 75,000 people in my senate district. How would you like to have a congregation that big?"

I believe now, more than then, that Christians are called to plunge into the life of the world, and to inject the moral and ethical values of our faith into the processes of governing. At the same time, there must be an absolute prohibition against granting any control by government over our religious freedoms. More recently, since our years in the White House, I have tended to move away from politics and toward religion, but the two are still related. There is no doubt that my having been a national political leader is what attracts most visitors to my Bible classes, and it is clear to me that many of these worshippers are eager to help shape our nation's political agenda.

In a speech to my fellow Baptists in 1978, I tried to explain the duality of my personal responsibilities as a president and a Christian:

> Thomas Jefferson, in the original days of our country, said he was fearful that the church might influence the state to take away human liberty. Roger Williams, who created the first Baptist church in America, was afraid that the church might be corrupted by the state. These

concerns led to our Constitution's First Amendment, which prohibits the establishment of any official state religion and, in the same sentence, prohibits the passing of any laws that might interfere with religious freedom.

Separation is specified in the law, but for a religious person, there is nothing wrong with bringing these two together, because you can't divorce religious beliefs from public service. At the same time, of course, in public office you cannot impose your own religious beliefs on others.

In my office at the White House I have to deal with many domestic and international problems: peace, freedom, nuclear explosives, the sale of weapons, terrorism, rapidly expanding populations without adequate food. But this is more than a list of political problems. These are also moral problems for you and me, because they violate the very precepts of God in which we believe.

I want our country to be strong enough in all elements, military and otherwise, so we never have to prove we are strong.

Reinhold Niebuhr, in his book Moral Man and Immoral Society, *pointed out the difference between a society and a people. The expectations from a person are a much higher standard. A person should have as our goal complete agape (self-sacrificial love). The most we can expect from a society is to institute simple justice.*

So, we as people have to do better, particularly if

we are blessed with the opportunity to demonstrate our worth. Leaders also must be careful not to be too timid. . . .

A country will have authority and influence because of moral factors, not its military strength; because it can be humble and not blatant and arrogant; because our people and our country want to serve others and not dominate others. And a nation without morality will soon lose its influence around the world.

What are the goals of a person or a denomination or a country? They are all remarkably the same: a desire for peace; a need for humility, for examining one's faults and turning away from them; a commitment to human rights in the broadest sense of the words, based on a moral society concerned with the alleviation of suffering because of deprivation or hatred or hunger or physical affliction; and a willingness, even an eagerness, to share one's ideals, one's faith with others, to translate love in a person to justice.

I was brought up in a family that was stable, cohesive, and remarkably isolated from the outside world, except for the small community of Plains, Georgia. Home was our unchangeable haven, in times of pain or pleasure. There was no doubt that my father made the final decisions, but we all knew that Mama's influence and opinions were always major factors in the management of our family. There were certain aspects of life, particularly in the running of the household and the raising of my sisters, that were almost exclusively my mother's purview. Together, our parents were dominant, and we children respected and obeyed them. In fact, I never deliberately disobeyed either of them. It was my mother, then my father, in whom I had absolute faith.

Nowadays, most Americans move around frequently and are exposed to many influences, and our environments and customs are multifaceted. But for me as a child, there were just a few sources of knowledge about myself or any other people. Our contacts with the world beyond our community were limited. We didn't have running water or electricity in our house, so time on the battery radio was restricted, even on the rare evenings when we stayed up after dark. On special nights, keeping our eyes fixed on the radio, we listened as a family to *The Lone Ranger, Little Orphan Annie, Fibber McGee and Molly,* and *Amos 'n' Andy.* My parents would sometimes let me stay up until 8:00 P.M. to hear Glenn Miller's band playing the current musical hits for fifteen minutes. That was all the outside world I knew. In addition to my family and our close neighbors, all African-American, I encountered other people just through school and the church in Plains. Our prom parties, which parents would support for entertainment and primarily to let boys and girls get acquainted in preparation for future marriages, were orchestrated by the church.

Sunday mornings were for Sunday School and preaching at Plains Baptist Church, where Daddy was a teacher and a deacon. I remember vividly that after church we always had the best meal of the week, usually fried chicken, mashed potatoes, hot biscuits, and vegetables from our big garden, followed by pies made from sweet potatoes or fruits of the season. Afterward, our activities were severely limited. There were no stores open, movies in the county seat were out of the question, and shooting a gun or playing cards was prohibited. Fishing in the nearby creek or pond was a close call, but eventually it came to be permitted if done discreetly. It would not have been appropriate, however, to walk down a public road with a fishing pole. My mother and father played cards, mostly bridge, but certainly not on Sunday. At the age of twelve, when I was deemed old enough to drive a car by myself, my sisters and I went back to the church on Sunday evenings for meetings of the Baptist Young People's Union (BYPU). This was very important, because it was the BYPU that sponsored most of the teenage social events. I need not go on, since the picture is fairly clear. It was a simple, family-centered, deeply religious, working existence, with interracial labor and play on the farm with my black neighbors. All the farmwork was done by humans or mules, and we grew corn as the common fuel for both. I imagine that, except for the radio, automobile, and a hand-cranked telephone, our lives were quite similar to those of our great-grandparents.

During those early years, I witnessed the racial discrimination that still survived almost a hundred years after the end of the Civil War. Mandatory segregation of black and white citizens was supported and enforced, at least in the Southeastern United States, by state and federal laws, and was not questioned by anyone of influence that I knew. The only person who paid no attention to these racial customs was my mother, and she treated everyone the same because, I presumed, she was a registered nurse and a member of the medical profession. When I was a child, all my friends and playmates were African-American, and the one who was preeminent at any time was whoever had caught the biggest fish, killed the most rabbits, or could run faster, jump higher, or pick the most cotton in a day. When I rode to our county seat with one of my playmates, we always sat in different railroad cars and at separate levels in the movie theater, attended different schools and churches, and I knew that white students rode in buses and black students walked to and from school. I do not remember knowing that only white adults were permitted to vote and to serve on juries.

My first awareness of how segregation affected me and my friends was when my playmates and I were about twelve years old, when we were leaving the field and approaching the barn through what we called the "pasture gate." The two black boys stood back to let me pass, and I presumed there was a trip wire there or some other reason for them to want me to go through first. Only much later did I realize that their parents had probably told them it was time for them to defer to me in some way. In a poem I wrote as an adult, I said,

INTRODUCTION

We only saw it vaguely then,
but we were transformed at that place.
A silent line was drawn between
friend and friend, race and race.

The next event that affected me directly was when I was a submarine officer and President Harry Truman ordained as commander in chief that all our military forces and the U.S. Civil Service end racial segregation. There was no trouble in implementing this command, and all of us on the ship saw the advantages gained by both black and white members of the crew. When our family returned home from the navy in 1953, this commitment to racial equality had become a part of our lives.

My father taught me that there should be a strict divide between religion and politics, and he also resented very deeply any intrusion of state or federal laws into our private affairs. I remember that Daddy opposed changing our clocks from "God's sun time" to "daylight saving time," and although a staunch Democrat in other elections, he never voted for Franklin D. Roosevelt after 1932, because the New Deal agricultural program provided, to stabilize farm prices, that half-grown pigs (shoats) should be slaughtered and that part of our growing crops of cotton and peanuts had to be plowed up. For many years afterward, Daddy recalled how difficult it was to force a trained mule to walk on top of a planted row to plow it up instead of in the middle to cultivate. I guess that today he would be known as a libertarian.

When I look back on my life, I can see how startling the changes have been. Eric Hoffer (1902–1983), the self-educated longshoreman and philosopher, described the years during my childhood as a time of hope, and the time of my adulthood as a time of desire. I knew the Great Depression years to be a time of hope, when the economic situation in America was so bad that everyone believed it could only improve; when things became plentiful, we tended to want not only what we already had but also what everyone else had.

Both at my presidential inauguration and when receiving the Nobel Peace Prize, I quoted my favorite teacher, Miss Julia Coleman, who summarized her advice on how to accommodate the uncertainties in our future: "We must welcome changing times, but cling to principles that never change." I would say that "cling to" meant "have faith in." I have thought often about Miss Julia's advice over the years, and especially during some of the most trying times of my life, when I had to decide which enduring principles should be applied to a particular event or situation, and sometimes I use it in my church and college classes and in counseling people who are distressed about current crises that we have to face.

Today, of course, family life even in the small Plains community is quite different. Some activities that were once strictly concealed in our "proper" society are probably no more prevalent but are now out in the open. Divorce has become acceptable, even for active church members. Without trying to analyze it too deeply, I see that one of the most significant changes is the relationship between young people and their parents. My siblings and I had an intimate and subservient relationship with our parents until we left home, but now the ties are substantially broken during the early teen years, no matter how much parents want to retain a strong influence over their growing children. The outside world is a much more powerful factor in life, with the availability of rapid transportation, television, social media, and particularly a broader circle of friends (and possibly rivals or adversaries), whose influence often exceeds that of immediate families. But perhaps just as many in today's world would still like to have certain faith in a core of principles that do not change. Where do we turn now when there is a moral question to be answered? What things in the twenty-first century are the same as they were eighty years ago? We still need a permanent foundation on which our lives can be fashioned. Without a central core of beliefs or standards in which to have faith and by which to live, we may never experience the challenge and excitement of seeking a greater life. We will have ceased to grow, like Jesus, "strong; he was, filled with wisdom, and the grace of God was on him" (Luke 2:40).

We must accommodate life's challenges, some welcome and others quite painful, but we don't want the verities of our lives to change. We need to have something unshakable in which to have faith, like a mother's love—something that can't be changed or destroyed by war, political events, the loss of a loved one, lack of success in business, a serious illness, or failure to realize our own ambitions. We need some foundation on which we can build a predictable and dependable existence.

This cannot always be found in either our nation's laws or our social customs. I would like to say as an American who has been president that the cherished values of our country are constant, but they are not. There are always powerful forces that work against the idealistic principles of peace, truthfulness, equality, justice, and even hospitality, freedom, and friendship. There is a lot of secret maneuvering that is never understood or even known by the public, and a great deal of unpublicized change in the interpretation of laws or the passage of new ones. Some laws violate what seem to be accepted principles and create serious divisions within our society. Also, almost every major religious faith—Catholic, Jewish, Protestant, Islamic—is divided over controversial secular issues like abortion, gay rights, the role of women in society, or even female clothing. But despite the confusion and controversy in secular affairs and among religious organizations, the basic principles I've just mentioned have never changed. These are the foundation for our faith.

People have always tried to improve their own lives, through communal living and the evolution of secular laws and rules considered to be beneficial, at least to a dominant portion of them. So far as I know, a concerted worldwide effort to encapsulate high ideals into a common agreement has been made only once, and included the nations who had been victorious, or at least neutral, in World War II. This common agreement is known as the Universal Declaration of Human Rights. I remember that I followed the United Nations proceedings in San Francisco very closely as a member of the U.S. Navy, either as a midshipman at Annapolis or from a battleship in the Atlantic Ocean. The key nations that founded the U.N. in October 1945 were the "Big Four"—China, the Soviet Union, the United Kingdom, and the United States—and they were joined by forty-seven others. The overriding objective was to prevent further armed conflicts after more than 60 million people had been killed in the war, and to agree on a set of peace incentives that could prevent warfare among future potential disputants. For many complex reasons, the United Nations's primary goal of preserving peace has not been reached.

Since that time, the military forces of our own country have been involved in conflict with more than twenty other nations, in wars that cost the lives of 10 million people, and the potential for further military engagements remains. As of November 2017, the United States military forces were actively engaged in Afghanistan, Iraq, Syria, Yemen, Niger, Somalia, Jordan, and Thailand. Andrew Bacevich, a retired colonel who lost a son in Iraq, made an accurate comment: "A collective indifference to war has become an emblem of contemporary America." One major reason for our citizens' lack of concern about warfare is that most families are not directly affected by these conflicts, since the burden of combat now falls on just the 1 percent of Americans who serve in the military.

To live in peace is only one of the key human rights, and in December 1948, when the General Assembly of the United Nations proclaimed the Universal Declaration of Human Rights, it described these principles in thirty brief articles. To the best of their ability, those who drafted this declaration extracted the highest moral and ethical ideals of the world's great religions and expressed them in secular terms that could be understood by lawmakers and private citizens of all nations. The Universal Declaration promised to all people the economic, social, political, cultural, and civic rights that underpin a life free from discrimination, want, and fear. As with the United Nations's promise of sustained peace, these promises of human rights have not been realized. It seems that there is a steady reduction in the number of things in which we can have faith.

We know that evolution is a global process, usually progressive, that results from the adaptation of living organisms to natural selection and sudden mutations. I believe it has been God's plan to evolve human beings, and that after thousands of centuries we now find ourselves uniquely endowed with an understanding of who and what we are and have the knowledge and freedom to help shape our own destiny. This freedom to help in affecting our future evolution is a great challenge and opportunity, and it is our inherited duty to contribute to moral and spiritual advancement.

It is sobering to realize that the average human intelligence has probably not changed appreciably during the last ten thousand years. In fact, the total capacity of the brains of Neanderthals has been found to be greater than that of modern humans. We also know that the process of learning has greatly accelerated during recent times with our improved ability to share information rapidly. For the first time, we have become aware that our own existence is threatened by things such as nuclear weapons and global warming. These recognized threats are, perhaps, already an ongoing test of our human intelligence, our freedom, and our ability to shape our own destiny. The human challenge now is to survive by having sustained faith in each other and in the highest common moral principles that we have spasmodically evolved, and through mutual understanding and peaceful cooperation in addressing the discerned challenges to our common existence.

It is urgent that humans take a new look at the rapidly growing need for the Universal Declaration of Human Rights, the Ten Commandments, the Koran, or the teachings of Jesus Christ and to see if these visions of improved human interrelationships might be used to meet the challenges of the present moment and evolve a future of peaceful coexistence, based on faith in each other.

– ONE –

Meanings of Faith

Now faith is confidence in what we hope for and
assurance about what we do not see. —Hebrews 11:1

Faith is not belief in spite of evidence but a life in
scorn of the consequences. —Clarence Jordan

Faith is the foundation of this book, and it is a rich, complex, even elusive concept. In its broadest secular meanings and also in a more specific reference to religious life, the word "faith" is profoundly important to all of us. When I completed my term in the White House and described the relationship I had tried to maintain with the people of America, I entitled my presidential memoir *Keeping Faith*. Fifteen years later, I wrote a book about the religious values and experiences that had shaped my life, and how the beliefs I inherited had been transformed into what I called *Living Faith*. It is obvious that my having kept faith with the citizens when I was in office and the faith that I have in my Creator and moral values are not the same. When I look for synonyms of the word, the short list includes (as used in *Keeping Faith*) "devotion," "loyalty," "commitment," "fidelity," "fealty," "dedication," and "allegiance"—and (as in *Living Faith*) "confidence," "trust," "reliance," "conviction," "belief," and "assurance." Since this book covers many of the same influences in my life, there is some inevitable similarity in the texts.

Both keeping faith and living faith have provided the foundation for our governments and great religions. Trusted leaders of ancient times defined those principles that described their highest ideals and expressed them in words and beliefs, and people agreed to adhere to them. The combined Declaration of Independence and the Constitution with its Bill of Rights would be a notable example for the people of the United States, while for Christians it would be the Ten Commandments amplified and further explained by Jesus Christ in his Sermon on the Mount. As already described, world leaders made a concerted attempt to reach the same goal following the Second World War, with the United Nations and the Universal Declaration of Human Rights.

These were supplemented by various international agreements, such as the Geneva Conventions, designed to protect wartime prisoners from torture or extreme punishment. In 1976 the International Covenant on Civil and Political Rights (ICCPR) and the International Covenant on Economic, Social, and Cultural Rights (ICESCR) were ratified by enough nations to become international law. I signed both covenants while president, and the United States finally ratified the ICCPR in 1992. Our country still has not ratified the ICESCR;

the American Convention on Human Rights, which I signed in May 1977; the International Convention on the Elimination of All Forms of Racial Discrimination; or the Convention on the Elimination of All Forms of Discrimination Against Women. Ours is the only country of 193 that has not adopted the Convention on the Rights of the Child. Since these global moves were effected, no important actions have been taken by the world community to improve the prospect of more equitable and humane relationships among people.

Instead, the disparity in wealth between rich and poor has increased greatly, the portion of Americans in prison has skyrocketed and now exceeds that of any other nation, the partisan and racial divisions among our citizens have become deeper and sharper, our democratic system of elections and governing has become a tool of the wealthy, and we no longer believe that the future for our children will be better than the life that we experience. Even more recently, the threat of nuclear war has become more acute, America has abandoned its leadership as champion of a clean and healthy environment, confidence in our elected leaders has deteriorated further, and we citizens have tended to lose faith in each other. Many of our citizens have also lost faith in other "principles that never change," including truth, equality, and goodwill.

These issues are of great concern to me as I enter the last stages of my life. I still have faith that the world will avoid self-destruction from nuclear war and environmental degradation, that we will remember inspirational principles, and that ways will be found to correct our other, even potentially fatal, human mistakes. My faith is the key to my optimism. It is important to understand what it means, because faith is involved in almost every aspect of our lives.

The first absolute faith that most of us developed was in our mothers, as we suckled at their breasts or relished the warmth of their protective bodies. Even as a child, I soon acquired faith in my father and later in my siblings, my teachers, some other relatives, and then a few of my close friends and playmates. I evolved faith in myself, with an increasing awareness of my own limitations. Later came faith in the U.S. Navy and fellow crew members on my submarine, plus things to which I was devoted during my career: democracy, freedom, and the ideals shared by citizens of the United States; service to others, justice, equality, and the truth. A simple example of faith is when we sing in a chorus or play in an orchestra, which requires an element of faith in one another, and a reciprocal need to cooperate. It is helpful to be reminded of the dictionary definition: "Faith is confidence or trust in a person or thing, or the observance of an obligation from loyalty, or fidelity to a concept, promise, or engagement." Faith involves each of us in a highly personal way, as an agreement or contract, a kind of devotion, confidence, loyalty, or reverence. Faith transcends what we learn from experience or from reasoning, but every human also retains the freedom to lose confidence in a thing or person and to break promises or oaths—even to violate marriage vows or to become a traitor to our country.

There is a difference between reasoning and believing, but both can lead to faith. "Faith" usually means belief either in a doctrine that we accept as truth or in a truth that is self-evident. We believe in things we never see, like historic events; ideals, like freedom; or the existence of germs and atoms. Sometimes we don't believe things we observe ourselves, like the apparent small size of stars and other heavenly bodies. There is much illusion and much expansion of our thoughts in the activity of believing or having faith. We like to understand what it is that we believe, and how and why we believe it. Immanuel Kant says that we have faith in something (a) because we have always believed it; (b) on authority that we respect; (c) by self-evidence; (d) through persuasion; (e) through reasoning; or (f) because it could encompass what our community accepts as real or true without discussion or dissension.

It is obvious that "faith" has many meanings, but it is most commonly considered to be religious in nature, and the best definition and examples of Christian faith are found in the eleventh chapter of the book of Hebrews:

Now faith is confidence in what we hope for and assurance about what we do not see. . . . By faith we understand that the universe was formed at God's command, so that what is seen was not made out of what was visible.

Because the Hebrew Bible does not focus on faith as belief, and assumes that all who read the Bible believe in God, the word "faith" is used only twice in the King James Version of the Old Testament and 245 times in the New Testament. The writer of Hebrews relates faith directly and by name to a number of biblical heroes of Old Testament times whose actions were determined by it.

By faith Abraham, when called to go to a place he would later receive as his inheritance, obeyed and went, even though he did not know where he was going. . . . By faith even Sarah, who was past childbearing age, was enabled to bear children because she considered him faithful who had made the promise. . . . By faith Abraham, when tested by God, offered Isaac as a sacrifice. He who had embraced the promises was about to sacrifice his one and only son. . . . By faith Moses' parents hid him for three months after he was born, because they saw he was no ordinary child, and they were not afraid of the king's edict. . . . By faith [Moses] left Egypt, not fearing the king's anger; he persevered because he saw him who is invisible. By faith he kept the Passover and the application of blood, so that the destroyer of the firstborn would not touch the firstborn of Israel. . . . I do not have time to tell about Gideon, Barak, Samson and Jephthah, about David and Samuel and the prophets, who through faith conquered kingdoms, administered justice, and gained what was promised; . . . whose weakness was turned to strength. . . . These were all commended for their faith.

The Bible goes on to say that "faith comes from hearing the message, and the message is heard through the word of Christ" (Romans 10:17); "A person is not justified by the works of the law, but by faith in Jesus Christ. So we, too, have put our faith in Christ Jesus that we may be justified by faith in Christ and not by the works of the law, because by the works of the law no one will be justified" (Galatians 2:16); "But my righteous one will live by faith" (Hebrews 10:38); "Do not think of yourself more highly than you ought, but rather think of yourself with sober judgment, in accordance with the faith God has distributed to each of you" (Romans 12:3); "We walk by faith, not by sight" (2 Corinthians 5:7); "You are all children of God by faith" (Galatians 3:26); "For it is by grace you have been saved, through faith—and this is not from yourselves, it is the gift of God—not by works, so that no one can boast" (Ephesians 2:8–9); "your faith—of greater worth than gold" (1 Peter 1:7); ". . . strengthened in the faith as you were taught, and overflowing with thankfulness" (Colossians 2:7); and "If we confess our sins, he is faithful and just and will forgive us our sins and purify us from all unrighteousness" (1 John 1:9). In fact, the Holy Bible is primarily about faith.

For humans to exist and live together and to share a common cause, we had to develop some degree of collective faith in each other, beginning within families and then extending to communities, villages, and ultimately to nations and even coalitions of nations. There can be disparities among them; citizens can be loyal to a nation, usually sharing common rules or laws, but it is not necessary for them to maintain personal faith in each other. Shared languages, beliefs, or interests help bind them together. We also submit to deities in which we have faith, out of our need for something or someone on whom to rely for meaning. I know from personal experience that faith in people or things can be a source of joy and strength and can help me meet challenges or accept times of sorrow or regret. Our faith is an integral part of our personalities.

Faith is always a living thing, which is usually shared with others. In fact, Richard Niebuhr said that when we hold something to be true, we always have a relationship to it through a person we trust. His exact words were "All knowing involves this triadic relation of at least two subjects and an object." To be a person is to be able to keep faith with each other, and Niebuhr's claim is that we are bound to each other only as we are mutually bound to some third reality, to a transcendent cause to which both owe loyalty and on which both depend. By necessity and in utilizing our human freedom, we recognize in each other a common loyalty and a common bond. His statement is somewhat difficult to understand, but it raises an interesting point for discussion.

The most important example of faith in my life has been

the marriage vows I exchanged with Rosalynn. I realize that marriages can be based on many things, like common interests, sexual satisfaction, a desire to have children, economic or social advantages, or just to evolve a family community. In every case, there must be a strong element of faith in one another, something like an agreement or contract. This shared commitment can be transcendent, requiring a leap of faith more binding than all others, designed to survive any future challenges or differences. At the time of our marriage we could have said, "I love you now, and I believe I will always love you and be faithful." Instead, we both took an oath before God "to have and to hold from this day forward, for better, for worse, for richer or poorer, in sickness and in health, to love and to cherish, until death us do part." Fortunately, our continuing love and faith in each other has made it possible to honor these pledges despite many differences and challenges.

We cannot remain true to ourselves if we are not faithful to those with whom we share a pledge, responsibility, or common cause. Faith implies, at least to some degree, a pledge of fidelity, and sometimes this can be at risk, or prove to be an error. There are occasions in our lives when we learn that our confidence in someone or in a concept no longer prevails. Marriages can prove to be ill-conceived, as can the formation of a close friendship, a business agreement, or a pledge of loyalty to an organization or an ideal. There are other limitations on faith. Sincere faith in something may not result in appropriate or commensurate action. For instance, we may accept and have total faith in the concept of racial and sexual equality, but we can then assume a superior relationship to others if it is to our advantage in dealing with blacks, Hispanics, or women, and act accordingly. The motivations for this response to a favorable opportunity usually come from an unattractive trait, like pride, envy, or selfishness.

Having genuine faith in something or someone almost always means that we will have a positive reciprocal action or a tangible response. We live by faith, always with trust in other people and in mutual causes or values that we adopt, such as equal status of people, the principles of democracy, the deleterious effects of lying, the value of an agreement or contract, or the shared benefits of justice and adherence to common laws. These kinds of principles can be understood and honored by expressing them in inspired language, like the American Bill of Rights, the Ten Commandments, or the Sermon on the Mount. Through them, we strive to comprehend and to improve ourselves and the world in which we live. Many of us associate reliance on a deity with the maintenance of an ideal structure of human relations. Interpersonal faith is the foundation for love and hope. If humans no longer have faith in each other, can we continue to exist?

TWO

Acquiring Faith

It is from the person of Jesus Christ that we
understand "the utterly transcendent and
otherwise hidden God." —Karl Barth

I love the recklessness of faith. First you leap, and
then you grow wings. —William Sloane Coffin

It is difficult to understand exactly where we get our faith, because it has multiple origins. I am convinced that all of us have
faith of different kinds, and that we can continue to expand
and strengthen the faiths that we enjoy. Each of us has at least
a modicum of faith in ourselves, and we develop a natural trust
in our parents and in other people on whom we depend for our
existence. This is quite different from our acquired faith in
God, science, or the value of democracy or education. Faith in
something can come from accepting the word of someone we
trust, or by a personal experience or a yearning for something
transcendent that gives us satisfaction or inspiration, helps explain mysteries of the universe, or perhaps gives meaning to

JIMMY CARTER

our lives. Most of those who encounter God do so first through the loyalty to God of parents, benefactors, and friends. It is an easy transition from faith in a person to faith in what that trusted person proclaims, and we quite readily have faith in something because the community around us has accepted it as unquestionable.

In adulthood, the truths from childhood are eventually tested and either accepted or discarded through our individual experiences or preferences. We learn to reason for ourselves, and usually depend less on the influence of other people. We evolve doctrines or premises that explain or give purpose to our lives, let us understand what we experience or observe, or accommodate our preferences. We are confronted with a multitude of choices and, on each occasion, we decide what is best for ourselves or what lets us comply with a previous overriding commitment. Many of these choices come naturally over time, but in some cases we decide deliberately and in advance what will be the objects of our faith.

Most people are influenced by religious faith, with statistics showing that about three-fourths of the earth's inhabitants profess to follow the teachings of Christianity, Islam, Judaism, Hinduism, or Buddhism, and most of the other believers worship ancestors, heavenly bodies, or some other aspect of nature. We submit to our deities out of longing for something or someone on whom to rely for meaning, or to perpetuate or strengthen an ideal set of morals or principles, such as peace, justice, equality, truth, kindness, compassion, or love. The rea-

— 34 —

son for studying a religion is not to decide if we wish to believe in it but usually to further understand or strengthen faith in what we have already adopted. We realize that perpetuation of our belief is dependent on transmission from one generation to the next, so proselytizing is an important factor for most believers.

Acquiring religious faith is a highly personal and subjective experience, possible only if we are searching for greater truths concerning ourselves and God. Despite periods of doubt, my own faith has been confirmed and strengthened by the tangible spiritual benefits I have received from the "confidence in what we hope for and assurance about what we do not see" (Hebrews 11:1). It is only through faith that I can maintain a livable relationship with the omnipotent Creator and my personal savior, Jesus Christ. Without this, I would feel destitute. The search for faith is challenging, even painful at times, but ultimately deeply rewarding. The life of faith provides answers to the most disturbing questions about our existence, the purpose of life, and how to deal with sorrow, failure, guilt, anxiety, and fear. Through faith we come to know that our gifts from God are not earned by our own acts but are given to us through God's grace and love. As Paul says, "Therefore, since we have been justified through faith, we have peace with God through our Lord Jesus Christ, through whom we have gained access by faith into this grace in which we now stand" (Romans 5:1–2).

Theologian Paul Tillich maintained that there is a profound difference between anxiety and fear. Anxiety, he wrote, grows out of the awareness of our own fragility, uncertainty, and impending death. By contrast, fear is of a specific, identifiable threat or object that can be faced or endured with courage. Tillich said that we should strive to change overwhelming anxiety into fear, with which we may deal more effectively. Our guilt and anxiety are relieved when we realize that God has already accepted us and loves us as we are.

My general attitude toward life is that of thanksgiving and joy, not anxiety or fear. In my weekly Bible lessons at our church, I teach that our Creator God is available at any moment to any of us, for guidance, solace, forgiveness, or to meet other personal needs. Prayer is also important to me. I pray often during each day, and I believe in the efficacy of prayer. Through prayer often comes self-assurance and the expectation of miracles. Prayer helps me internally, as a private conversation with my Creator, who knows everything and can do anything.

Our former pastor Dr. Dan Ariail used to say that God responds to prayer by saying "Yes," "No," or "You've got to be kidding!" If I were an amputee, for instance, my prayer would not be to restore my leg but to help me make the best of my condition, and to be thankful for life and opportunities to be a blessing to others. At the moment, we are monitoring the status of my cancer, and my prayers about my own health are similar to this. God is not my personal valet. God does not build a protective fence around my life, keep me from trouble, fulfill my personal desires, or guarantee my success. However, through prayer God offers me comfort, reassurance, satisfaction, courage, hope, and peace.

How we think about God is critically important for the life of faith. Some theologians, including Paul Tillich, have said that God is not a being, but being itself. I disagree. I believe that through prayer I have a direct and personal relationship with God as a specific entity, and I believe that God knows and understands me. My relationship to God is not based on hearsay, but it is highly personal, and this intimate relationship affects my moral values and my behavior.

Acquiring faith is not an easy or frivolous thing. All of us would like to have an absolutely certain base on which to build our lives. For a Christian, the Bible is that base. It tells us about our Creator, how to use our personal freedom, and how to forge a life of purpose, joy, and peace. It speaks to questions of life after death, our relationships to other people, and how to deal with sorrow, failure, fear, temptations, and the lack of love in our lives. But how can we fathom the creation of the universe? How do we discern the meaningfulness of life or the mystery of love? When these bewildering questions absorb me, I fall back on my faith as a Christian. It is foolish for me to think that my doubts can change the truth, which must always be in harmony with my faith in God.

As a believing Christian, I have no problem with discoveries in astronomy, geology, and paleontology: that the universe is enormous and expanding, that the earth is ancient, and that human beings have evolved from primitive ancestors. It is not difficult for me to accept the "big bang" theory of the origin of the universe, at least until it is refuted by further scientific exploration of the heavens and new explanations are evolved to explain what God has done. Nor does it shake my religious faith to realize that the early authors of the Scriptures thought that the earth was flat, that stars were little things like Christmas tree ornaments that could fall on us, that the entire process of creation occurred during six earthly days, and that the first woman came from the rib of the first man, with both Adam and Eve created in modern human form. The gap between their understanding and ours just indicates that truths that had always existed were revealed later to Galileo, Newton, Darwin, Einstein, and Hubble—and to most of us.

Many years ago I wrote a poem on the subject:

A Contemplation of What Has Been Created, and Why

I tried to fathom nature's laws
From twirling models and schoolroom sketches
Of molecules and parts of atoms,
And nearly believed—but then came quarks,
Bosons, leptons, antiparticles,
Opposite-turning mirror images,
Some that perforate the earth,
Never swerving from their certain paths.
I've listened to conflicting views

About the grand and lesser worlds:
A big bang where it all began;
Of curved, ever-expanding space;
Perhaps tremendous whirling yo-yos
That will someday reach the end
Of cosmic gravity and then
Fly back to where they can restart
Or cataclysmically blow apart—
And then, and then the next event.
And will it be an accident?

I am sure that none of this is an accident. If Paul expected ancient Christians to believe in God because of their relatively limited observations of the world around them, shouldn't our faith be stronger, especially since we know so much more about God's creation?

In its own way, technology offers a lesson in the nature of faith, with plenty of things in modern life that we believe but can't understand. The computer, radio, television, space travel—all once seemed miraculous, but most of us now accept them as routine. We can set up an antenna and bring in 250 different television programs. The waves are all around us, plus countless radio signals, waiting for us to extract them from the ether for our pleasure or information. There is no way for us to detect in advance that the signals are here, or for most of us to explain how these electromagnetic waves can be changed into music or colored, moving pictures almost instantaneously.

These are amazing things that few of us comprehend, but we believe them.

Faith comes to us personally and individually as a gift, and not as the result of a deliberate effort to understand in order that we may believe. There are many religious concepts I cannot fully understand; even some aspects of the life of Christ remain mysteries. Among these are the extremes of love and sacrifice, power and weakness, the demand for perfection along with total forgiveness, the omnipotence of God personified in a human Son who wept and was tempted to be sinful. The totality of it is overwhelming, but I accept it with confidence—through faith. We have an innate desire to relate to the all-knowing, the all-powerful, and the ever-present—to some entity that transcends ourselves. We want to know that our lives are meaningful. At the same time, faith has to be predicated on a desire to believe. The Leonard Cohen song about Christ's walking on the water says Jesus knew that "only drowning men could see him." Faced with death, in a storm, the disciples wanted to believe. I have always felt that my own faith has been made possible or strengthened by my sincere desire to have it, a personal blessing to me.

There is a discussion among Christians about the sufficiency of faith in our relationship with God. Some see the acquisition of faith as the end of the process, while there are others who consider ministering to the poor, the despised, and the homeless as important elements of our faith. The first group often looks upon the second as less than truly Christian, sometimes using the phrase "secular humanist" to describe them. I have been faced with this charge. In 1980 a high official of the Southern Baptist Convention came to the Oval Office to visit me when I was president. As he and his wife were leaving, he said, "We are praying, Mr. President, that you will abandon secular humanism as your religion." This was a shock to me, especially when I learned that he was referring to "human beings who are capable of being ethical and moral without religion or a *god*."

Later, I discussed this encounter with our pastor at First Baptist Church, and he surmised that it was because I had made presidential decisions that contradicted political positions espoused by leaders of the newly formed Moral Majority and other groups of conservative Christians. I had appointed many women and minorities to high positions in government, rejected using government funds for religious education or private schools, established an independent department to enhance public education, failed to overturn the *Roe v. Wade* abortion decision of the Supreme Court, and normalized diplomatic relations with the Communist government of China. I had also called for a Palestinian homeland, supported the Equal Rights Amendment, negotiated with the Soviet Union on nuclear arms control and other issues, and espoused human rights and failed to use our military as a key element in promoting American interests overseas. I could not deny any of these analyses.

Another thing I had done after becoming president that

had displeased some other Christians was to end the practice
of having religious services that I personally sponsored or en-
dorsed. As early as 1966, I had led a Billy Graham crusade
in my home county, and I was honorary chairman and had
participated in his Atlanta crusade when I was governor. Although President Nixon and some of my other predecessors
had invited Billy Graham to speak to groups and to pray in the
White House, I decided that this was not appropriate.

In 2002 I expressed my growing concern about some aspects of fundamentalism. In replying to a query on the subject
from *Christianity Today,* I wrote:

> *There is a remarkable trend toward fundamentalism in
> all religions—including the different denominations of
> Christianity as well as Hinduism, Judaism, and Islam.
> Increasingly, "true believers" are inclined to begin a
> process of deciding: "Since I am aligned with God, I am
> superior and my beliefs should prevail, and anyone who
> disagrees with me is inherently wrong", the next step
> is "inherently inferior", the penultimate step is "subhu-
> man," and then their lives are not significant.*
>
> *That tendency has created, throughout the world,
> intense religious conflicts. Those Christians who resist
> the inclination toward fundamentalism and who follow
> the nature, actions, and words of Jesus Christ should
> consider people who are different from us to be worthy*

of our care, generosity, forgiveness, compassion, and un-selfish love.

It is not easy to do this. It is a natural human inclination to encapsulate ourselves in a superior fashion with people who are just like us—and to assume that we are fulfilling the mandate of our lives if we just confine our love to our own family or to people who are similar and compatible. Breaking through this barrier and reaching out to others is what characterizes a Christian and what emulates the perfect example that Christ set for us.

In *Our Endangered Values: America's Moral Crisis,* published in 2005, I listed some characteristics of fundamentalism:

1. *Almost invariably, fundamentalist movements are led by authoritarian males who consider themselves to be superior to others and, within religious groups, have an overwhelming commitment to subjugate women and to dominate their fellow believers.*

2. *Although fundamentalists usually believe that the past is better than the present, they retain certain self-beneficial aspects of both their historic religious beliefs and of the modern world.*

3. *Fundamentalists draw clear distinctions between themselves, as true believers, and others, convinced that they are right*

and that anyone who contradicts them is ignorant and possibly evil.

4. *Fundamentalists are militant in fighting against any challenge to their beliefs. They are often angry and sometimes resort to verbal or even physical abuse against those who interfere with the implementation of their agenda.*

5. *Fundamentalists tend to make their self-definition increasingly narrow and restricted, to isolate themselves, to demagogue emotional issues, and to view change, cooperation, negotiation, and other efforts to resolve differences as signs of weakness.*

To summarize, there are three words that characterize this brand of fundamentalism: pride, domination, and exclusion.

In sharp contrast, Jesus espoused humility, servanthood of leaders, and breaking down walls between people.

Our faith should be a guide for us in deciding between the permanent and the transient, the important and the relatively insignificant, the gratifying and the troubling, the joyful and the depressing. We sometimes study the principles on which our faith is founded, but we must not become obsessed with the belief that we have a special ordination from God to interpret the Scriptures and to consider anyone who disagrees with us wrong and inferior. The tendency of fundamentalists in Christianity and other religions to condemn those who differ from them is perhaps the most disturbing aspect of their current ascendancy. One of the worst sins is pride and the belief that we are good enough to look down on others. I guess it is human nature for nations, classes of people, or even individuals to set their own standards and mores and then to find themselves to be good. Karl Barth says that religion is our search for God, and that this always results in our finding a god that is most convenient for our own purposes. He distinguishes this from Christian faith, which results from God's seeking us through Christ.

When people become alienated from one another, it is important to search for a healing force. A husband and wife may have a child who can hold them together. Members of an athletic team who don't really like one another will cooperate in the heat of a game. Our faith in God should play such a unifying role among believers. This may seem obvious, but all too often we forget or ignore it.

– THREE –

Religious Faith

When God speaks and we respond with faith, we are
born into a new life. —Rudolf Karl Bultmann

The Christian faith finds the final clue to the meaning
of life and history in the Christ whose goodness is
at once the virtue which man ought, but does not,
achieve in history. . . . From the standpoint of such
a faith it is possible to deal with the ultimate social
problem of human history. —Reinhold Niebuhr

Most of the religious part of this text is based on my preparation and teaching of Bible classes ever since I became an adult.
When I was a midshipman at the U.S. Naval Academy, I
taught the children whose parents were stationed there. Later,
while serving on ships, I conducted religious services on special
days, such as Christmas and Easter. A dozen or more of the
submarine crew would sit on folding bunks between the torpe-
does, and I would stand forward in the torpedo room close to
the launching tubes to read the religious text, ask and answer

some questions if I could, and say a prayer. After I left the navy and returned home to Plains, Georgia, my wife, Rosalynn, and I taught young boys and girls in Sunday School regularly for about fifteen years, as my father had done when I was a child. Even when I was president, while we were members of Washington's First Baptist Church, the regular teacher and I would set aside a few Sundays each year for me to teach the adult class, without informing the public in advance.

Today, in Plains, I lead a Bible class at Maranatha Baptist Church, a congregation of about thirty active members, many of whom have lived and worshipped together for several generations. ("Maranatha," meaning "Come, Lord," is the first Christian prayer of which we have any record, from 1 Corinthians 16:22.) Since most of our adult members are teaching their own classes, keeping the nursery, or managing other affairs of the church, almost all my students are visitors. There are usually several hundred people who come to worship with us, including busloads from other churches or vacationers who stop by on journeys to or from Florida. Rosalynn and I have photographs with those who remain for the pastor's sermon (and the morning collection). Quite often, some will whisper to me that they have never been in a church before, or not since they were baptized as babies.

My personal library contains a good collection of books about philosophy, religion, and theology, and I refer to them quite often as I prepare my Sunday lessons about my Christian faith. I have just a rudimentary knowledge of the other major religions whose members are often represented in my classes, including Jews, Muslims, Buddhists, and Hindus, but they are always welcomed and sometimes participate in the discussions. I am somewhat familiar with Judaism because about half the lessons I teach are from the Hebrew text of the Bible. I have also spent hours trying to understand the basic Islamic beliefs during the Iranian hostage crisis and more recently in our work with Muslim leaders to minimize abuse of women and girls that is caused by misinterpretation of the texts from the Koran and the Holy Bible. While carrying out projects of The Carter Center, I have learned what I could from long talks with religious leaders about Hinduism in Nepal and Buddhism in Myanmar.

One of my most memorable discussions about religious faith was when I was governor of Georgia during the 1970s. Bob Dylan gave a concert in Atlanta, and I invited him and his band members to the mansion after the concert. My three sons were very excited to spend time with the band, and I was pleased when Bob asked for a private discussion with me. He and I went out into the garden, and for an hour or so I answered his questions about my Christian faith. I did my best to respond accurately and fully, but I did not attempt to convince him that he should change his own Jewish beliefs. It was very interesting to me to contemplate his intense personal interest in the subject after he announced his Christian faith in the late 1970s. I have attended several of his concerts since then, and I went to Los Angeles to present the MusiCares Person of the

Year award to him in February 2015. The event was excit-
ing, and the array of performers was impressive, with Willie
Nelson, Neil Young, Bruce Springsteen, Norah Jones, Sheryl
Crow, Bonnie Raitt, Jack White, Tom Jones, Crosby, Stills &
Nash, and many others all singing Dylan songs as a tribute to
him. One of the comments I made was "His words on peace
and human rights are much more incisive, much more powerful, and more permanent than those of most Presidents of the
United States." After thanking me, Bob gave an interesting,
rambling thirty-five-minute talk about his career and his personal relations—both good and bad—with other performers.

The similarities and differences among the world's major
religions are too complex to explain here, but it can be seen that
Christianity, Judaism, and Islam are closely related. Their combined believers now comprise at least 4 billion people, approxi-
mately half the population of the earth. I spent many hours at
Camp David in 1978 discussing with two other devout men,
President Anwar Sadat and Prime Minister Menachem Begin,
the fact that our three different faiths all look upon Abraham's fidelity to God as a basis for our own beliefs, and that
we also share a reverence for Moses. Sadat always emphasized
that Muslims join Christians in revering Jesus Christ. There
remain many theological disputes among our three religious
groups, especially relating to the status of Muhammad and
Jesus. We agreed that the primary modern competition was
between Christians and Muslims, both of whom are dedicated
proselytizers. Although Hindus and Buddhists have different

bases for their beliefs, they share many of the same moral goals of personal behavior and treatment of others. Believers in any of the great religions can find a lot in common. I am sure we also have atheists, agnostics, and other nonbelievers who join our worship services at Maranatha, but they usually refrain from revealing their lack of religious faith to me. These sessions also include representatives from a dozen or so Christian denominations, sometimes including Quakers, Mormons, Mennonites, and Amish. Most of the American states are usually represented, and a number of foreign countries. Because of this diversity, I've had to consider other people's questions and concerns, some of which have never been raised in my own life.

Most of the time, it is a pleasure for me to study the suggested Scripture, consider how best to present the lesson, read some commentaries, and try to connect the Bible subject with current events, even when the issues are controversial. I have learned that the best way to deal with a complex theological issue or a difficult Bible passage is to involve the class in a give-and-take discussion, which keeps us all awake and helps us understand the subject. We have lively debates but few injured feelings. Some of the exchanges continue after the services are over, even in letters that come to me during the following weeks. I have also discovered during these years of teaching that it is better for me to avoid preaching or lecturing and to assume that we are all exploring the meaning of the text on an equal basis. This, I might add, is in keeping with my Baptist heritage. Baptists do not have theological authorities mandating how we must interpret Scripture or what we must believe. The more memorable times in the classes at Maranatha are when we have the feeling of a community of people striving to decipher the meaning of the Bible verses and applying the message to our own lives and to current events. My similar hope is to maintain an equal or shared relationship with the readers of this book, so that we can search together for the many meanings of faith, how they relate to us, and perhaps how they can affect our lives in a positive way.

Why does religious faith exist? One reason that some deities have been created is out of fear that the creators' existence will end at the time of their physical death, which they know from experience to be always imminent. We also create our gods to fill a longing for something or someone on whom to rely to evolve and sustain an ideal set of morals or principles. Religious faith always rests primarily on a divine content and foundation.

I was startled when I first contemplated Luke 18:8, which asks, in effect, "When Jesus Christ returns, will he find faith on earth?" I don't know if this question is about our future faith in God or our faith in each other and in the principles that shape and guide almost every aspect of our lives. I wonder if humanity can survive without faith in ourselves, in one another, or in the basic principles of life. Can the moral values of democracy, freedom, justice, equality, and compassion be transmitted to a next generation without religious faith? I hope so, but I am confident that religious faith enhances the possibility of that transmission.

It is possible in talking about faith to substitute law for the spirit of the law. Without denying the value of the older law, Jesus gave six specific examples of higher standards than the laws of Moses. These are known as the "antitheses" (Matthew 5:21–46).

> *You have heard that it was said to people long ago, "You shall not murder, and anyone who murders will be subject to judgment. But I tell you that anyone who is angry with a brother or sister will be subject to judgment."*

> *You have heard that it was said, "You shall not commit adultery." But I tell you that anyone who looks at a woman lustfully has already committed adultery with her in his heart.*

> *It has been said, "Anyone who divorces his wife must give her a certificate of divorce." But I tell you that anyone who divorces his wife, except for sexual immorality, makes her the victim of adultery, and anyone who marries a divorced woman commits adultery.*

> *Again, you have heard that it was said to the people long ago, "Do not break your oath, but fulfill to the Lord the vows you have made." But I tell you, do not swear an*

oath at all; either by heaven, for it is God's throne; or by the earth; for it is his footstool; or by Jerusalem; for it is the city of the Great King. . . . All you need to say is simply 'Yes' or 'No'; anything beyond this comes from the evil one."

Ye have heard that it was said, "Eye for eye, and tooth for tooth." But I tell you, do not resist an evil person. If anyone slaps you on the right cheek, turn to them the other cheek also."

You have heard that it was said, "Love your neighbor and hate your enemy." But I tell you, love your enemies and pray for those who persecute you.". . . If you love those who love you, what reward will you get? Are not even the tax collectors doing that?"

Another troubling relationship debated throughout the Bible is between faith and works. The two are closely intertwined and inseparable, but I believe and teach that genuine faith is preeminent, as shown in these verses: "For it is by grace you have been saved, through faith—and this is not from yourselves, it is the gift of God—not by works, so that no one can boast" (Ephesians 2:8–9). However, James (the half brother of Jesus) questions the sincerity of those who might claim to have faith but lack the commensurate results: "What good is it, my brothers and sisters, if someone claims to have faith but has no deeds? Can such faith save them? Suppose a brother or a sister is without clothes and daily food. If one of you says to them, "Go in peace; keep warm and well fed," but does nothing about their physical needs, what good is it? In the same way, faith by itself, if it is not accompanied by action, is dead. But someone will say, "You have faith; I have deeds." Show me your faith without deeds, and I will show you my faith by my deeds" (James 2:14–18). Jesus also emphasizes the importance of good works as a result of faith, especially in the twenty-fifth chapter of Matthew, when he says, "Then the King will say to those on his right, "Come, you who are blessed by my Father; . . . For I was hungry and you gave me something to eat, I was thirsty and you gave me something to drink, I was a stranger and you invited me in, I needed clothes and you clothed me, I was sick and you looked after me, I was in prison and you came to visit me." . . . "Whatever you did for one of the least of these brothers and sisters of mine, you did for me." Paul addressed this question in his letter to the believers in Rome: God "will repay each person according to what they have done" (Romans 2:6).

There is also a long-standing debate between science and religion, which I consider to be fruitless and unnecessary. The purpose of science is to reduce the extent of what is unknown, while religion stresses the fact that there are important aspects of life that cannot be directly observed or otherwise proven. As a Christian who has also studied nuclear physics and delved into the mysteries of space, I have not detected any conflict between science and religious faith. One of my favorite books is

Rocks of Ages by Stephen Jay Gould, a famous scientist and prolific writer with whom I exchanged letters as we argued about facts or principles. He believed, as I do, in evolution of species and in proven scientific facts about cosmology and geology. He explained that the "Magisterium" of religion concerns itself with the ultimate meaning of life and moral values. Scientific discoveries, on the other hand, reveal ever more truth about the awesome character of God's creation, as scientists have explored among fossils and developed microscopes, telescopes, and the ability to learn more about nature. I realize that scientists may never unravel the full truth about God's creation, with 95 percent of the universe composed of undetectable dark matter and energy. For those of us whose religious faith is firm, no scientific fact that might be learned can contradict God.

Unlike other living creatures, humans are capable of self-reflection, of worship, and of morality; humans can envision or desire a better or ideal life, have knowledge of coming events including mortality, and are able to judge ourselves. We can envision things that have never happened and imagine how these occurrences might affect us. These unique characteristics are interrelated. For instance, having knowledge that we will die, we are inclined to revere a transcendent entity that offers us some protection against being nonentities subsequent to the end of our known existence. The basic moral codes that shape and control our lives are the results of the laws of evolution; they have not varied for ages, and we know that their preservation is always dependent on transmission from one generation to the next. Primarily because of the tools and weapons that ensure our dominance, our physical development of strength and agility is no longer important in competition with other animals for survival. This means that the course of ascending evolution will be shaped by whether we learn to cooperate in doing what is good for each other instead of how we can prevail over others in combat.

I believe this means that humans will have to evolve and implement fair and equitable treatment among ourselves, which could come close to the Universal Declaration of Human Rights. Almost always, when we seek security in things, we find that we are in competition with our neighbor. In effect, our developing moral concepts (such as in the Ten Commandments) put an end to the previous vital factors in evolution: for each of us to live, procreate, and to survive we had to engage in killing, stealing, lying, and doing whatever else was necessary for our own survival and well-being. Our personal responsibility is to strive to do better, perhaps to reach for moral and ethical goals that at times seem to be out of reach. This is the realm of religion, so this means that we must be free of restraint by others in order to be such innovative activists. The aim of most religions has been to preserve our highest ideals, apply them to current circumstances, and of course extend them to as many people as possible. Religion is never based on science, or things that we know as fact, but always based on moral concepts or visions of something superlative or idealistic. Not "I believe what I observe about God" but "I believe *in* God and I relate to God personally. This helps to enhance my moral ideals and my behavior."

In answering the members of one of the earliest Christian churches who asked him about the things on which they could depend if they adopted the Christian faith he espoused, Paul wrote: "So we fix our eyes not on what is seen, but on what is unseen, since what is seen is temporary, but what is unseen is eternal" (2 Corinthians 4:18). The things we cannot see are paramount, even though we can see only their effects of peace, truth, justice, equality, forgiveness, or love. Paul followed up by reminding the same congregation, "For we live by faith, not by sight" (2 Corinthians 5:7). Religious faith is a belief in something that has always existed; it is never based on scientific discoveries, or what we learn as facts, but always on a moral concept or a vision of something superlative or idealistic.

To me, God is the essence of all that is good, and my faith in God induces a pleasant feeling of responsibility to act accordingly. I remember that a Basque Christian author, Miguel de Unamuno (1864–1936), wrote: "To believe in God is to desire His existence, and what is more, to act as though He existed." My concept of God helps me comprehend the purpose of my life, as well as explain the creation of humans and the origin of our universe. Jesus is worshipped not because he was perfect and without sin but because God was present in him. He personified what God meant for us humans to be. Jesus does not come to us just through the Scriptures but directly in all the encounters of our lives. For a Christian, the constant access to God and the life and teachings of Jesus offer a sound moral foundation that includes all the most basic ideals that should guide and inspire us. Since these highest standards are eternal and apply to everyone, we have an obligation to comprehend what they are and what they mean. Our faith can provide enough knowledge and courage to apply these lessons to our daily lives. If specific guidelines or examples are not always available, at least our basic values can help narrow the options. For me, sharing any problem with God through what can be a quick and silent prayer provides a powerful element of calm and objectivity. Then, when I might fear or regret the consequences of a choice I have made, an awareness of the presence and love of God can give me courage. John says that Christ knows us all (John 2:24), and Paul reminds us that nothing can separate us from the love of God (Romans 8:39).

I have faced some difficult personal challenges, as have almost all other people. I have had to confront physical danger, financial despair, feelings of guilt, family tragedy, political failure, and quandaries, concerning my career. In almost all such crises, thorough analysis of the problem combined with prayer has been at the heart of my response. Prayer is the most essential element here. Even when I have been reluctant to reveal my challenges and unanswered questions to any other human being, including Rosalynn, I was always able to share them with God. Prayer helps me analyze the problem I face and understand myself, including those things that are buried deep within me. This opens up a very important healing process.

Unfortunately, I don't always exploit the assurance my Christian faith offers. Sometimes I go a long way down the road in a quandary, suffering inside, before finally I ask myself, "Why don't I talk to God about it?"

When I pray in such times, I try to ask myself some key questions: "Am I pursuing the right goal?" "What would Jesus do?" And, finally, "Have I done my best, based on the alternatives open to me?" If I then make the best possible decision I can, things often work out well. But if I've tried everything I can and still fail, I find that I can say, "So be it," putting the remaining problem in God's hands. This gives me a degree of equanimity that lets me live with the outcome, whatever it may be.

Scientists have argued about whether the existence of God can be proven by the basic laws of thermodynamics. The first law states as simply as possible: "Energy can be neither created nor destroyed, but can only be converted from one form to another." The second law of thermodynamics, which Albert Einstein said is "the premier law of all science," states that this available energy is constantly changing into more unavailable forms, and can be expressed also as "The universe is constantly getting more disorderly and chaotic." To summarize their theological argument, some scientists explain that in the entire universe as a closed system, we know that heavenly bodies are cooling down as they lose energy into space. In another, even more simple analogy, the entire universe is winding down like a giant clock. Since energy is continually changing from available to unavailable forms, someone or something not bound by the second law of thermodynamics had to give it its maximum available energy in the beginning (or to wind up the universal clock). Only the creator of the second law of thermodynamics could violate it.

Here are some scriptural references and comments that I have personally found worthy of contemplation:

> *Karl Barth: "God is free in his judgment and it falls on himself (Jesus); so that man would be free from judgment; the situation of every man has been changed by the death and resurrection of Christ. The peace treaty has been signed."*

> *Saint Augustine: "Our hearts are restless until we find rest in God."*

> *"If you believe, you will receive whatever you ask for in prayer" (Matthew 21:22).*

> *"Let us draw near to God with a sincere heart and with the full assurance that faith brings, having our hearts sprinkled to cleanse us from a guilty conscience and having our bodies washed with pure water" (Hebrews 10:22).*

> *"For in Christ Jesus . . . the only thing that counts is faith expressing itself through love" (Galatians 5:6).*

– FOUR –

Demonstrating Our Faith

There is no such thing as Christian faith apart
from Christian conduct. —Emil Brunner

You should read the Bible in one hand and your
newspaper in the other. —Karl Barth to students

I have met many famous people of deep religious faith, including Mother Teresa, Pope John Paul II, Nelson Mandela, Archbishop Desmond Tutu, Anwar Sadat, Menachem Begin, and Billy Graham, some of whom have had a direct and beneficial effect on my life. There is another kind of faith, perhaps more difficult to sustain: having a firm belief in yourself and in other people, or in a seemingly impossible dream. Most often, but not always, these people also have deep faith in a religious cause. I would like to describe a few of these close acquaintances.

Millard and Linda Fuller

For the past thirty-five years, Rosalynn and I have spent at least one week each year building homes for poor people in need. Habitat for Humanity is "seeking to put God's love into action, bringing people together to build homes, communities, and hope," and it was founded by Millard Fuller and his wife, Linda. As students at the University of Alabama, Millard and a partner, Morris Dees (later founder of the Southern Poverty Law Center), started several innovative ventures. One was the publication of cookbooks featuring the best recipes from the mothers of other students, and another was delivering cakes or flowers to students on birthdays or other special occasions after their parents had been contacted by Fuller and Dees. After graduation, Millard married Linda and began to practice law, but he had so much money coming in from his other business ventures that he gave up his law practice. One day, much to Millard's shock, Linda told him that she was leaving him and going to New York for marriage counseling because he was neglecting his family and seemed interested only in getting rich. Millard followed her, begged her to come back to him, and finally agreed to give away all his money and join Linda in any work they could share.

Millard kept his promise, and the couple soon settled on the biracial Koinonia Farm, just a few miles south of Plains, Georgia, and began building houses for destitute black families. Then they and their three children spent three years in Zaire as missionaries supported by some Christian groups, and they developed the idea of organizing Habitat for Humanity, using the "theology of the hammer" or the "economics of Jesus." This was a dream that few people believed could be realized, but working with volunteers and homeowners, Habitat has now built or renovated more than 2.5 million homes in a total of seventy countries. One of the Habitat staff members told me, "Millard has the dreams, and then we inherit the nightmare of fulfilling his vision."

Volunteers work side by side with families who have been living in subhuman dwellings. The future homeowners are chosen and most other decisions are made by committees formed within the local community. There is no charity involved, if "free handouts" is the meaning of "charity." The homeowners must contribute about five hundred hours of work on their own and neighbors' houses, and repay the full price of their homes, to which they have clear title. This can be done because the houses built by Habitat are relatively inexpensive, much of the construction work is done by volunteers, and Habitat's policy is not to charge interest. These conditions make monthly payments possible from a low income, or even a monthly welfare check. It is difficult to describe the emotions of our Habitat workdays, where we see extraordinary commitments and lives changed among formerly forgotten people. The deep Christian faith, vision, and dedication of Millard and Linda Fuller have also helped to change our lives.

The Ethredges

In 1976, the same year I ran for president, Jerome Ethredge was an agronomist at the experiment station near Plains. Active in the work of our local church congregation, Jerome and his wife, Joann, realized that their faith was leading them to a fuller and more challenging life. With no previous religious experience except as lay members of our church, Jerome and Joann volunteered for full-time service as Baptist missionaries. After receiving instruction and French-language training, they were assigned to Togo, in West Africa. The ministry of Jerome and Joann provides a vivid demonstration of the inseparability of religious faith and good works.

For seven years the Ethredges served in a large city, where they offered language and other education courses to young people who were willing to visit their small Christian library. Hundreds learned to read and write, but few had any interest in the religious aspect of the center. In time, Jerome and Joann decided they wanted to move to a small town in the East Mono region, where the needs were great and they could use Jerome's experience in agronomy. Most of the people there worshipped various aspects of nature, and all attempts by both Muslim and Christian evangelists in this region had failed. Within sixty miles of their new home, there were only five small Muslim and two Catholic congregations. Jerome and Joann decided to combine Christian witnessing with attempts to alleviate the people's urgent physical needs.

One of the most obvious needs was for drinking water. Most villages were near a water hole that filled during the rainy season and provided only stagnant water the rest of the year, bringing disease to those who drank it. Many other people lived miles from any water supply, and women had to walk as far as sixteen miles each day to fetch clay jars of water, alternating this duty with others who cared for all the children and performed the rest of the community chores. With financial support from some Baptists in North Carolina, Jerome began to dig wells with a truck-mounted diesel drill. He had to penetrate a regional layer of granite at or near the surface, making the operation slow and tedious. Assisted only by the local residents, he went to every village within eighty miles of his home base and ultimately drilled 167 wells, 130 successful and capped with donated hand pumps, until all villages had a clean and healthy water supply.

During this time, Jerome also used his farming skills to increase the production of basic food crops. Recognizing the shortage of protein in the villagers' diets, he acquired a bulldozer and constructed twenty-one deep ponds that filled during the rainy seasons. The ponds were stocked with tilapia fish, and they now provide a continuing source of food. While Jerome was busy with these and other projects, Joann worked with families on intensive health and education projects. She helped to build a pharmacy and arranged transportation to a distant regional hospital for people too ill to be treated locally.

The greatest remaining problem of the East Mono people was that, except for a long and circuitous route, they were isolated from the rest of Togo during four months of the rainy season, when the Mono River became an impassable torrent. Only one small dugout canoe, hewn from a tree trunk, was available to cross the river in emergencies. Working again with local people and his Baptist friends from North Carolina, some of whom came to Togo as volunteers, Jerome designed and eventually built a bridge across the river. Rosalynn and I were amazed when we visited the Ethredges to find a 230-foot concrete span. It was hard to believe that this vital transportation link had been built by one missionary and some volunteers.

When the Ethredges left Togo after twenty-three years of service, there were eighty-one church congregations in East Mono, each with a trained pastor, with a total of five thousand active members. All this work was done in a quiet and self-effacing way, in complete cooperation with the Togolese people, and always in the name of Christ. The Ethredges demonstrated their faith by their work in classrooms and health clinics, behind ox-drawn plows, on hospital trips in a dilapidated van, on a bulldozer, or operating a borehole drill.

Bill Foege

The first major health conference we convened at The Carter Center was named Closing the Gap. We had more than 125 public health specialists in attendance, and we learned that two-thirds of all deaths before the age of sixty-five were preventable, provided people had the knowledge, access, and financial means to invest in health. Relatively rich people had these means but died unnecessarily young because of smoking, excessive drugs and alcohol, obesity, lack of exercise, and other personal choices. The orchestrator of this meeting was Dr. Bill Foege, a dedicated Christian who had devised the procedure that led to the eradication of smallpox. When I was president, I appointed him director of the Centers for Disease Control (CDC). After he led the groundbreaking project for The Carter Center, I convinced him to become our executive director. Rosalynn and I wrote a book about the findings of our conference entitled *Everything to Gain: Making the Most of the Rest of Your Life.*

Bill helped to devise our Center's health programs, with a goal of addressing neglected tropical diseases that were the primary cause of suffering and death among some of the poorest and most deprived people on earth, caused not by obesity, drugs, alcohol, or lack of exercise but by contaminated drinking water, lack of sanitation, exposure to insects or leeches, ignorance, or lack of basic health care. With unwavering faith in his own ability, the wisdom and dedication of suffering people who are eager to improve their own lives, and faith in the efficacy of public health, Dr. Foege helped launch programs against dracunculiasis (Guinea worm), onchocerciasis (river blindness), trachoma, schistosomiasis, lymphatic filariasis (elephantiasis), and malaria. Throughout his career as a world leader in public health, Bill has inspired his fellow workers and towered above his peers in achievement and in stature (he is six feet seven inches tall).

Bill Foege is known as a prankster and raconteur, believing that all of us need humor in our lives. When he was fighting against smallpox in Biafra, in the eastern region of Nigeria, the priority challenge was to immunize hundreds of people scattered in small, isolated villages. He went to see the regional chief, explained the program, and asked for a guide to take him to the widespread communities. The chief looked up at the tall American and replied, "No, it will be easier if we bring them all here." He directed his drummer to commence sending a message, and the next morning a stream of people crowded into the village square. After they were immunized, Dr. Foege asked the chief, "How in the world did you induce them to come here just for an immunization program?" The chief replied, "I told them to come if they wanted to see the tallest man in the world." The Americans and Africans were sitting around a campfire that night, and Bill asked the chief how detailed a message he could send by drums. The chief summoned his drummer and whispered some instructions, and the drummer beat out the message. On the far side of the arena, a tribe member took the pen from his shirt pocket and brought it over to give to Bill—as the drummer had instructed.

Bill later became chief medical adviser for the Bill & Melinda Gates Foundation, and was awarded the Presidential Medal of Freedom in 2012. Bill Foege is one of the great heroes of my life, and he continues to play an important role in the work of The Carter Center.

Annie Mae Hollis Rhodes

When I was growing up on a farm in Archery, a young woman named Annie Mae Hollis worked for my parents. After I left home for college, she moved to Albany, Georgia, where she married a man named Rhodes and got a job helping in a wealthy woman's house. When my father was terminally ill, Mother called Annie Mae and said, "I can't nurse Earl and take care of all the family at the same time. Could you come back and help me?" So Annie Mae moved back to Plains to be with our family. I will never forget that when my father breathed his last breath, on July 22, 1953, Annie Mae Rhodes was holding him in her arms.

Annie Mae had a good life. Because of her sterling qualities, she never lacked a job, and she became almost a full member of the families she served as a maid. She was a stalwart member of her church and a counselor to others in her congregation. She owned her small but attractive home, which was a focal point for socializing, especially among her church family. Her handicapped brother lived with her, able to move around, mostly in his wheelchair, and even assist in the household chores. In July 1994, Annie Mae was sleeping when, in the middle of the night, her brother woke her and said, "It's been raining for hours, and the radio says the water's coming." She said, "The water's not coming. I've been here thirty-seven years, and water's never come in my house." But he insisted, so she got up, found her Bible, and tried to pull her old dog out of the house. Before she could get to the car, the water was waist deep, so she clung to the car door handle until some rescue workers picked her and her brother up in a boat. Her dog drowned, and her car, her house, and everything in it were destroyed. Annie Mae lost all she had, except a Bible and the small and now water-ravaged lot where her house had stood.

Rosalynn and I were in Japan when we heard about the flood, and we didn't know anything about Annie Mae's plight. Two women from Atlanta went down to Albany within a couple of days to help in the relief work, and they met this extraordinary old woman, who was hobbling around trying to see what was left of her community. She was helping to rejuvenate everybody's spirits by saying, "We need not be concerned. The Lord will take care of us. We have to have faith in God and in ourselves." The two women were so impressed with Annie Mae Rhodes's faith that they asked about her life. She mentioned in passing that she had worked for our family about forty years ago, but she said, "Don't bother Mr. Jimmy. I don't want to be a burden to him." Nonetheless, the women wrote me a letter and described what had happened. Some of us volunteers with Habitat for Humanity helped Annie Mae build a small, new house on her lot. She decided, since she was elderly and didn't have any children, and since her brother was also quite old, to deed the house back to Habitat when she passed away.

Annie Mae's simple faith, expressed in works, was what

James described in his New Testament epistle: "Consider it pure joy, my brothers and sisters, whenever you face trials of many kinds, because you know that the testing of your faith produces perseverance. Let perseverance finish its work so that you may be mature and complete, not lacking anything" (James 1:2–4). Most of us don't know from personal experience how people like Annie Mae Rhodes live in potential floodplains, the ghettos of America's cities, or the Third World nations of Sierra Leone, Ethiopia, Haiti, Niger, or Chad. But James tells us to let our religious faith inspire us to help alleviate their suffering.

"Enduring faith" described Annie Mae Rhodes, who survived the flood that destroyed her home. Hundreds of flood victims, Habitat volunteers, and other rescue workers were inspired by the quiet faith of a stooped, confident, quiet seventy-seven-year-old woman.

Hyman Rickover

Except for my father, Admiral Hyman Rickover is the man who has had the greatest impact on my life. Born in Poland in 1900, he was brought to the United States by his Jewish parents at the age of six. He was a graduate of the U.S. Naval Academy and did advanced work in electrical engineering at Columbia. Shortly after marrying, Rickover wrote to his parents of his decision to become an Episcopalian, remaining so for the rest of his life. He served with distinction during

World War II, and *Time* magazine featured him on the cover of its January 11, 1954, issue. The accompanying article described the man I knew during the years I served under him: "Sharp-tongued Hyman Rickover spurred his men to exhaustion, ripped through red tape, drove contractors into rages. He went on making enemies, but . . . he also won a reputation as a man *who gets things done*." After arousing the animosity of many senior officers, Rickover was put in charge of developing nuclear power plants to propel ships, and in 1950 I was an eager volunteer to serve in this program.

Rickover interviewed me with a withering array of increasingly difficult questions and finally asked how I stood in my Naval Academy class. I responded, "Sir, I was fifty-ninth in a class of 820." Then he asked, "Did you do your best?" I started to say, "Yes, sir," but I remembered who this was and recalled many times at the academy when I could have learned more about our allies, our enemies, weapons, strategy, and seamanship. I was just human. I gulped and finally said, "No, sir, I didn't always do my best." He looked at me for a long time, and then turned his chair around to end the interview. Over his shoulder, he asked one final question, which I have never been able to forget—or to answer. He said, "Why not?" I sat there for a while, shaken, and then slowly left the room.

After a few days, I was selected by Rickover to be commanding officer of the crew that helped design and build the power plant for the second atomic-powered submarine and was sent to Schenectady, New York, where General Electric was the contractor. During the months ahead, Rickover never said a kind word to me, like "Good job" or "Well done," or thanked me for my work. His silence was the greatest sign of approbation. No matter how he drove his subordinates, we all knew that he demanded even more from himself. I would sometimes fly with him from the East Coast to visit the Hanford plant in Washington State, where nuclear fuel was refined. Before jet planes, this was a journey of ten or twelve hours, first to Seattle and then back to Richland. Determined to make a good impression on my boss, I would resolve to work all the way. Despite my best efforts, I would have to take a brief nap, but Rickover never rested. I never discussed religious faith with him, but Rickover had exemplary faith in his own ability and judgment, the value of tenacity, and the ultimate triumph of scientific facts.

It was only while I was president that he became polite and friendly. He never requested any White House favors, and I realized that, as always, he did his utmost to accomplish his extremely challenging duties. Rickover's high and stringent standards are responsible for the U.S. Navy's continuing record of zero reactor accidents, while during the same time the Russians had fourteen nuclear disasters. In addition to designing nuclear plants for propelling ships, he was a pioneer in evolving low-cost and safe nuclear plants for producing electricity.

As president, I accompanied him on sea trials of a new nuclear submarine, and he said that since nuclear weapons had become so threatening, he would prefer that atomic power had never been discovered. When I was in a position of power, it caused me concern that some people who worked for me compared me to Rickover. I overheard one of them say about me, "When we make a decision to do something, we begin looking for a calendar, but Carter looks at his watch."

Lillian Gordy Carter

Lillian Gordy moved from Richland, Georgia, to nearby Plains in 1922 to become a registered nurse. She married Earl Carter the next year, and they became my parents in October 1924. Lillian first worked at a hospital in Plains and was paid four dollars a day for twelve hours on duty, which was a substantial boon to the couple's income. When my father became a farmer with a little more income, Mama began nursing in the homes of our African-American neighbors and took care of others who were poor and needed help. She was supposed to receive six dollars for twenty-hour duty but rarely collected full pay during the Great Depression years. After Daddy's death, in 1953, Mama was housemother of a fraternity at Auburn University for seven years, then managed a nursing home until she "got tired of being around old folks," and joined the Peace Corps at the age of sixty-eight. She nursed in a clinic in Vikhroli, India, a village owned by the wealthy Godrej family. I wrote a poem based on one of her letters to us children:

Miss Lillian Sees Leprosy for the First Time

When I nursed in a clinic near Bombay,
a small girl, shielding all her leprous sores,
crept inside the door. I moved away,
but then the doctor said, "You take this case!"
First I found a mask and put it on,
quickly gave the child a shot and then,
not well, I slipped away to be alone
and scrubbed my entire body red and raw.
I faced her treatment every week with dread
and loathing—for the chore, not the child.
As time passed, I was less afraid,
and managed not to turn my face away.
Her spirit bloomed as sores began to fade.
She'd raise her anxious, searching eyes to mine,
to show she trusted me. We'd smile and say
a few Marathi words, then reach and hold
each other's hands. And then love grew between
us, so that when I kissed her lips
I didn't feel unclean.

The Godrejes' gardener secretly brought Mama flowers
and vegetables, and told her that he had a son and daughter
but that he could not afford to send his daughter to school.
Having no other way to repay him, my mother taught the little
girl how to read and write, and about the world outside. Mama

served in India for two and a half years, then returned home and made more than five hundred speeches before her death fifteen years later. She spoke about how good the Peace Corps service was and said, "We are never too old to serve." The U.S. Peace Corps now gives an annual Lillian Carter Award to the former volunteer who served after the age of fifty and has exhibited the most admirable service to others.

Later, Rosalynn and I led a group of Habitat volunteers in building a hundred homes near Vikhroli, and the Godrej family had a reception for us and invited some of the people who had known Mother. I asked what happened to the gardener's daughter, and she stood and told us that she was now president of the region's university.

Mama was a deeply religious woman, and she followed the parable of Jesus by making full use of every talent and opportunity to serve others.

Ugandan Missionaries

One of the most memorable examples of faithfulness I ever knew occurred early in my term as president, when I found myself at odds with Idi Amin, the military dictator of Uganda. A few years earlier, the U.S. ambassador in Kampala had declared Amin's regime to be "racist, erratic and unpredictable, brutal, inept, bellicose, irrational, ridiculous, and militaristic" and our American embassy there had been closed. I do not remember having mentioned Amin in any of my public statements, but he was described in American news media at the time as being one of the world's worst human rights oppressors, with the International Commission of Jurists estimating the number of Ugandan people killed by him to be about 300,000, including a former prime minister, the chief justice of the supreme court, and the Anglican archbishop. In any case, Amin strongly condemned my human rights policy and threatened to retaliate. About a month after my inauguration, he issued an edict that no American could either enter or leave Uganda, and that all our citizens who were living in his country had to personally meet with him. I contemplated moving some warships into the region and began contacting any friendly foreign leaders who might have influence with Amin. After a few days, he announced that all Christian missionaries were under arrest, and that if I did not apologize for critical American comments about him, some of the missionaries would be executed. I learned that he was a Muslim and had great respect for the leaders of Saudi Arabia, so I asked Saudi King Khalid to intercede. He did so, and Amin then announced that all the captive Americans would be permitted to leave Uganda. None of them chose to do so, and they returned to their village posts and continued with their Christian ministry.

Billy Carter

Although I have already extolled my mother, I consider my younger brother worthy of special mention. Billy was quite different from me, and superior in many ways. Mama always said that he was the most intelligent member of our family, and none of us who knew him well ever disputed her. Two of his most outstanding characteristics were his ability to make friends and his remarkable sense of humor. I have never formed more than a few close and intimate friendships at a time, and I would estimate that Billy usually had ten times as many. As a member of our family, he became an object of interest to the many news reporters who flooded into Plains when my presidential campaign progressed, and they were fascinated with Billy's gregarious behavior. One of them asked him if he considered himself to be peculiar. After a moment, he replied, "Look, my youngest sister is a Holy Roller preacher, the other one spends half her time on a motorcycle, my mother joined the Peace Corps when she was about seventy years old, and my brother thinks he is going to be President of the United States! Which one of us do you think is most normal?"

The reporters were complimentary at first, but many of them became highly critical later in his life. Billy became an apparently hopeless alcoholic while I was president, but twelve years before his death Billy decided on his own, encouraged by his wife, Sybil, to combat his addiction. He never drank again, was reconciled with his family, and lived a full and productive life. During these years, he and Sybil traveled all over America to inspire thousands of addicts who were struggling to break their dependence on alcohol and drugs. Impressed by Billy's humorous and down-to-earth account of his own travails and his faith in their ability to follow his example, they responded with surprising enthusiasm to his beneficial counseling. Successfully fighting his desire for alcohol through all those years, Billy demonstrated his self-confidence, or faith in himself.

On his deathbed, surrounded by close friends and family and knowing he was afflicted with pancreatic cancer, he was still able to fill the room with laughter. My brother was an inspiration to me.

FIVE

What Faith Means to Me

*Man is a living soul . . . but as one who cannot live
except as he lives by faith.* —Richard Niebuhr

*Faith means the betting of one's life upon the
God in Jesus Christ.* —Søren Kierkegaard

Throughout my ninety-three years, my faith in other people, concepts, and things has provided necessary stability as I have enjoyed mostly happy times and gratifying accomplishments. As an adult, I moved from a naval career to farming, to business, to politics, and, since the end of my presidency, to a challenging and enjoyable life as a college professor, a private citizen with worldwide interests through The Carter Center, an author, an aspiring craftsman and artist, and to the mostly pleasant responsibilities of a senior citizen with a large family. I have been blessed with a loving and enduring marriage and have attained many of the goals I set for myself as a young man. Some of my career changes were of my own choosing, and others have been forced on me by what I considered at the time to be disappointments or complete failures. Throughout these years, my faith as a Christian has provided the necessary stability in my life. Come to think of it, "stability" is not exactly the right word, because faith in something is an inducement not to dormancy but to action. To me, "faith" is not just a noun but also a verb.

I have come to realize that I have not been involved in some of the most important decisions that shaped my life. I had nothing to do with my having been born, the identity of my parents or where I was raised, what talents or abilities I have, or the gift and responsibility of human freedom that I enjoy. Except for suicide, I do not have the freedom to decide when my life will end. I also will lack any power to decide if I continue to exist after my body no longer lives. I believe that God determines my existence and destiny. I realize that my physical strength and endurance are steadily declining, and I am having to learn how to conserve them, but I have found with relief and gratitude—even when facing the prospect of an early death from cancer in my liver and brain—that my faith as a Christian is still unwavering and sustaining. I spend more time in prayer now than in former years, mostly in an attitude of thanksgiving rather than supplication.

A commitment to my basic Christian faith was instilled in me in childhood. I had the double influence of a church environment and my own father as my Sunday School teacher. My religious faith at first was simple and unequivocal; there was no doubt in my mind about the truth of what I learned in church. But even in those early years I was dismayed to find myself becoming skeptical about some aspects of my inherited faith. We learned in church that Jesus had risen from the dead three days after his crucifixion, and that all believers would someday enjoy a similar resurrection. As I grew older, I began to wonder whether this could be true. I became quite concerned about it, worried not so much about the prospect of my own death as about the possibility that I might be separated from my mother and father. These two people were the core of my existence, and I couldn't bear the idea that I would not be with them forever. By the time I was twelve or thirteen years old, my anxiety about this became so intense that at the end of every prayer, until after I was an adult, before "Amen" I added the words "And, God, please help me believe in the resurrection." What made it worse was that I thought I was the only person with such concerns. I felt guilty that I doubted what the preacher said, what my father taught me in his weekly Bible class, and what I assumed our church members all accepted without question. I believed I was watched by a punitive God and would have to suffer for my lack of faith. Unfortunately, I never let my father know about my skepticism, because this was not the kind of thing we would have talked about at home.

Although other doubts about my faith have arisen, I have eventually overcome them by prayer, study, and a strong desire to believe what I have accepted as an integral part of my existence and a never-realized ambition for my own behavior. For me, this ideal behavior is based on the life and example of Jesus Christ—not because of his perfection but because he represents God in human form and helps me understand my proper relation to God and to other people. At the same time, I try not to judge the faith of either other Christians or those of a different inspiration, because to do so contradicts the admonition of Jesus: "Do not judge, or you too will be judged."

Like Paul, I see the glory of God's creation around me, in the unfathomable mysteries of the universe and the diversity and intricacies of creation. I stand in wonder at how a tree grows from an acorn, how a flower blooms, or how DNA can shape the appearance and character of a living creature. It is almost humanly incomprehensible that in our Milky Way galaxy there are billions of stars equivalent to our sun, and then billions of other galaxies like ours. At the other end of the scale, I marvel that the "inseparable" atom I learned about in high school is really a collection of remarkable components, matter and antimatter, rotating in different directions yet held together by forces of immense power, and that some particles pass through the entire earth without being deflected.

Equally miraculous is the human form, in which the billions of neuron connections in a single human brain almost equal the number of stars in the Milky Way. Over the centuries, scientists have discovered more and more about these truths—truths that have always existed. None of these discoveries contradicts my belief in an ultimate and superior being; they simply strengthen the reverence and awe generated by what has already become known and what remains unexplained.

There was an organized group of doubters in America who claimed to be searching for the "historical" Jesus. Some of them visited my home for discussions, and I have read their claims that most of the New Testament accounts of the life and teachings of Jesus are false or greatly distorted. Rudolf Bultmann discounted claims like these as worthless and unnecessary. He believed that it was not important if the authors of the Gospels got some details wrong. Since most people who knew Jesus during his lifetime did not believe in him, one should not be surprised that some modern-day skeptics find it difficult to believe. This group also emphasized the disparities that exist among some of the Gospel accounts, and many people point out Jesus' lack of any tangible accomplishments that might equal those of Muhammad, who was a powerful warrior, created a lasting empire, and transmitted the Koran from the angel Gabriel to his many believers.

I have the 1989 edition of a book named *The 100,* which ranks the most influential people in history, and the author, Michael Hart, places Muhammad at the top, ahead of Jesus. Hart explains, "There are two principal reasons for that decision. First, Muhammad played a far more important role in the development of Islam than Jesus did in the development of Christianity. Although Jesus was responsible for the main ethical and moral precepts of Christianity, St. Paul was the main developer of Christian theology, its principal proselytizer, and the author of a large portion of the New Testament. Furthermore, Muhammad (unlike Jesus) was a secular as well as a religious leader. In fact, as the driving force behind Arab conquests, he may well rank as the most influential political leader of all time." I can understand why many Muslims have become devout followers of Muhammad, and I am reassured to realize that most of the highest moral principles are common to these two great religions and to others.

It is not possible to dispute the book's statements about Muhammad or to name any great personal accomplishments that would gain historical fame for Jesus Christ. He was described by the prophet Isaiah as the coming Messiah—a "suffering servant" who would be physically unattractive, scorned, and rejected. As the story of the temptations of Jesus in the desert shows in the fourth chapter of Matthew, he refused to reveal miracles that would exalt himself or demonstrate his own greatness. Instead, when he performed extraordinary acts of healing that would have increased his fame and recruited followers, quite often he would say to the person he had just cured, "Don't tell anyone what I have done." He was a humble servant instead of a military conqueror, and we know him as the "Prince of Peace," who even loved his enemies. During his ministry he had no money, few possessions, and no home; he was alienated from the members of his own family; he was abandoned by his closest friends and followers in the time of his arrest, conviction, and execution; and he died as a common criminal when he was still a young man. How could this be the one I worship?

I have come to realize that the apparent weaknesses of

Christ are really what make him precious and give him a quality of authenticity that is convincing. Even the discrepancies among the four Gospel writers in describing details of his life's history make it easier for me to have faith in the Scriptures. If they had been contrived accounts, the early Christian leaders would have eliminated all the disparities. I try to absorb the essence and meaning of the direct teachings of Jesus Christ, supplemented by the letters written by Paul to the early churches. When there are apparent discrepancies, I decide what to believe, respecting the equal status and rights of all people.

I believe that if Jesus had been miraculously saved from death and triumphant over his persecutors, then his being on earth, even with his reported words and miracles proven by indisputable evidence, would have been of no lasting consequence. He has entered the life of the human world as the most persistent of rulers, the most cherished companion of all. Jesus Christ reveals and explains God, as God reveals and explains Jesus. The Christian faith exists because of Jesus and what he meant to his followers, and because he continues to live within the 2 billion believers who have faith in him and who know him in our personal lives. His most cherished message to me is that nothing can separate me from the love of God. I do not remember any time when Jesus was absent from my life. He explains the true character of the God of love and reassures us that ultimate power on earth will be good, not evil. It is through God and his Son that I strive to understand the world in which we live.

I am convinced that Jesus is the Son of God, and that he personified as a human being all that is good. I am not a Christian because I think that belief in Christ will make me popular, wealthy, or influential, or let me live after death and see my parents and my family again. Those are not major considerations for me anymore, although some of them were important earlier in my life. What is crucial is what Christ means to me as a personal savior, an avenue to understanding God my Creator, an exemplary personal guide for a way for me and others to live, and a constant source of reassurance, strength, and guidance.

After some thought and contemplation of written definitions, I consider myself to be an evangelical Christian. According to my Bible commentary, "Evangelism is the active calling of people to respond to the message of grace and commit oneself to God in Jesus Christ." Wikipedia says that "evangelicals believe in the centrality of conversion or the 'born again' experience in receiving salvation, in the authority of the Bible as God's revelation to humanity, and in spreading the Christian message." The basic elements of Christianity apply personally to me, shape my attitude and my actions, and give me a joyful and positive life, with purpose.

I was surprised a few years ago to realize how important it is for people to comprehend that our lives have a clear purpose and to know what our higher calling might be. A public opinion poll in *USA Today* asked: If you came face-to-face with God, what question would you ask? The top four responses were "How long will I live?" (6 percent); "Is there intelligent life elsewhere?" (7 percent); "Is there life after death?" (19 percent); and "What is my purpose in life?" (34 percent!).

As a Baptist, I believe in the "priesthood of believers," which means that every individual Christian has constant and direct access to God, and that neither our local preacher nor any other person needs to be involved. Also, we consider each of our churches to be completely independent of a superior organization or authority; we choose our own pastors, and any decision of the church is made exclusively by a majority vote of our own members in conference. I have retained these same religious beliefs, which were shared with the Southern Baptist Convention (SBC) until a more conservative group acquired practical control of the convention and adopted some guiding principles with which I did not agree. These new policies led, in effect, to the imposition of a creed that became binding on all Southern Baptist churches, members, committees, and SBC agencies and institutions, and it resulted in the prohibition of women as pastors, military chaplains, deacons, and at times the teachers of male students. While conservative SBC leaders deny it, SBC churches were all expected to accept the same basic principles and practices as adopted at the annual SBC conventions. These included an understanding of foreign missions that minimized social ministries (like that of the Ethredges), a reinterpretation of the priesthood of believers that exalted the pastoral role, the exclusion of women as pastors, and a denunciation of gay rights.

After leaving the White House in 1981 and seeing the growing divisions among Baptists, I tried to restore harmony by convening two meetings at The Carter Center, each comprising about forty of the top Baptist leaders, seven of whom had been or would become presidents of the Southern Baptist Convention. These efforts ultimately failed, and I was relieved when more moderate (or traditional) Baptists formed the Cooperative Baptist Fellowship (CBF), where we found a new home and which now has about 1,900 affiliated churches. The international organization of our denomination is the Baptist World Alliance, formed in 1905 and including about 48 million members, which the CBF has joined and from which the SBC has resigned.

The heated discussions and animosities that were generated during this brief period of dispute have largely dissipated, and Baptists are now grateful to realize that the basic affirmations of our Christian faith were not shaken. These traditional Baptist convictions continue to shape our attitude and actions, and give us joyful and positive lives, with the same commitments and ideals.

I experienced a relatively dormant phase in my religious life during the seven years I spent in the navy after marriage. With assignments to four different ships at naval bases in Virginia, Hawaii, California, and Connecticut, it was not convenient for Rosalynn and me to be part of a single nurturing church community. However, I sought out opportunities to worship when and where I could. For instance, when I got off duty on Sunday mornings after a week or two at sea, I would almost always find a Christian church service to attend on the naval base, even though I was eager to get home to my family. It did not matter to me what kind of service it was—I attended either Protestant or Roman Catholic services, and took communion at both—I just went to whichever service was earliest, so I could get home sooner.

I was enjoying a burgeoning navy career when I was called home to my father's deathbed. This proved to be a turning point in my spiritual life. During the days before and after my father's death, my immersion in the Christian community of Plains was an overwhelming experience for me. I felt that I had a family with several hundred people in it instead of just five. This was something I had almost forgotten since I'd left home as a teenager. Questions returned about my religious faith, however, and they were more intense because of losing my father. This was the first real tragedy in my life. I had lost my grandparents earlier, but I had not been very close to them. I found my father's death hard to understand. How could a good man, not nearly as old as many others in Plains, be deprived by God of his productive life? It seemed to me a harsh act, one I could only attribute to what I thought of as the God of the Old Testament, a stern, judgmental figure, very different from the loving, forgiving Jesus I knew from the Gospels.

This is when I began to explore in some depth the writings of theologians. I had attended four different universities without ever taking a course in religion or theology, but now I began buying books by authors like Dietrich Bonhoeffer, Rudolf Bultmann, Karl Barth, Martin Buber, Paul Tillich, Pierre Lecomte du Noüy, Hans Küng, and particularly Richard and Reinhold Niebuhr, and I began to read and examine their ideas. Later, when I was president, I mentioned that I found Reinhold Niebuhr's ideas to be especially helpful, and I was pleased several weeks later when his widow, Ursula, sent me a collection of his taped sermons.

My reading of theology, which helped open new ideas about faith for me, was an illuminating experience in which I began to feel at ease with my religion for the first time since I was a small child. I explored more deeply the relationship between religion and my scientific knowledge, my continuing doubts about the biblical accounts of miracles, and my impression of a conflict between a harsh and punitive God and a gentle and loving Jesus. I came to realize that it was a mistake not to face my doubts boldly and with an open mind. A torturous time of searching followed as I struggled to understand and differentiate among the varying explanations of faith and the nature of God that I found in the works of theologians and philosophers. I was searching for a point of view with which I could feel comfortable. I considered fellow worshippers in our local church who never seemed to lack absolute faith to be the lucky ones.

The turning point for me was the realization that there was

no difference between the God of the Old Testament and the God of the New Testament, between the perfect love of Jesus and that of God the Creator. I was reminded of the Bible verses that had always stressed this truth, such as when Jesus said, "Anyone who has seen me has seen the Father" (John 14:9), and when the apostle John wrote, "God is love" (1 John 4:8). It has been challenging and mostly enjoyable for me to face my doubts and questions and to seek answers through prayer and study. I am no longer afraid that opening the door to questioning might shake the foundation of my faith or anger God. Sincerely desiring to have faith, I have been able to correlate in my own mind the basic religious beliefs that I have expressed in this book.

Only one other time in my adult life was my Christian faith severely tested, while at the same time I lost confidence in myself. The two were closely related. Up until 1966, I had been successful in reaching all my major goals. I had received a valuable education, earned a good reputation in the navy, been blessed with a wonderful marriage, and completed two productive terms in the Georgia State Senate. Quite confident that year, I ran for governor of Georgia, but when the election was over I had come in third. Complying with the state constitution, which stipulated that if no candidate received a clear majority of the votes the legislature was to make the determination, they chose Lester Maddox, an avowed segregationist, to occupy the new governor's mansion. His proudly displayed political symbol was a pick handle that he used to drive potential black customers from the door of his restaurant in Atlanta. I am embarrassed now to admit that I was so proud and arrogant that I could not believe God would let this person prevail and become the governor of our state. Heartbroken and discouraged, I felt my life was a failure, and I was disillusioned about my religious faith.

My youngest sister was Ruth Carter Stapleton, at that time a very successful and famous evangelist who had written five inspirational books and made speeches to large audiences in America and in many foreign countries. She was especially noted for being able to express her Christian faith in a highly intimate and humble way, and her daily ministry was giving help individually to people who suffered from alcoholism, drug addiction, mental illness, marital problems, or other afflictions. Ruth drove down from her home in North Carolina to comfort me, and she listened patiently while I bemoaned my misfortune, deplored the poor judgment and racist tendencies of my fellow Georgians, and vented my anger toward God. Then Ruth told me that the disappointments of life should be accepted with happiness and anticipation.

I said, "Ruth, my political life is over! It's not my goal just to grow peanuts, sell fertilizer, gin cotton, and build up a bank account. I have nowhere to go! God has rejected me through the people's vote."

Ruth replied, "Jimmy, you have to believe that out of this defeat can come a greater life."

I responded with bitterness, "Ruth, you and I both know

that this is nonsense. There is no way I can build a worthwhile future on such an embarrassing defeat."

Then she referred to the passage from James: "Consider it pure joy, my brothers and sisters, whenever you face trials of many kinds, because you know that the testing of your faith produces perseverance. Let perseverance finish its work so that you may be mature and complete, not lacking anything. Blessed is the one who perseveres under trial because, having stood the test, that person will receive the crown of life that the Lord has promised to those who love him" (James 1:2–4, 12).

Patiently, Ruth explained that if I would retain my simple faith I could find a way to use my apparent failure as a step toward success in the eyes of God. She asked me if I had ever really gone out of my way to try to fulfill my obligations as a Christian, and I remembered a recent sermon in our local church that had been troubling to me. I didn't remember anything the pastor had said, but I couldn't forget the sermon's title in the church bulletin: "If you were arrested for being a Christian, would there be enough evidence to convict you?" I admitted that I could probably talk my way out of any such legal accusation. After all, my claiming to be a Christian had certainly been helpful in my business and in my political life. After some more discussion, she advised me to search for a way to serve others for a while, and not be so preoccupied with my own ambitions.

Ruth encouraged me to do something extraordinary, something totally unrelated to my business or to politics. I didn't know what this might be, but shortly afterward I was asked by the Baptist Brotherhood to go to Lock Haven, Pennsylvania, where I would work under the influence of a more experienced partner as a lay witness on a pioneer mission. This turned out to be a farmer from Texas named Milo Pennington, and our assignment was to visit in the homes of about a hundred families who were not members of any church, describe to them the advantages of accepting our Christian faith as a way of life, and explain the step-by-step "plan of salvation." In very basic and abbreviated terms, it is "All of us fall short of the glory or perfection of God, and deserve punishment. But God loves us, and through his grace—not because we have earned it—God offers us complete forgiveness if we have faith in Jesus Christ. In his crucifixion, Jesus has taken our punishment, and through repenting and accepting this forgiveness we are reconciled with God and can now have eternal life, with the Holy Spirit dwelling within us."

In Lock Haven, I soon learned that the results of our visits were not dependent on our presentations, but that we just had to do the best we could, relax, and have faith in the Spirit of God. More than forty people became Christians, and a small church was started. This experience changed my religious life forever! We stayed in Lock Haven until we finished our assignment, and the next year I was sent to Springfield, Massachusetts, and at later times to some racially changing areas of Atlanta. We devoted our time in Springfield to visiting families from Puerto Rico, so I used my limited Spanish to advantage. My companion this time was Eloy Cruz, the Cuban pastor of a small church in Brooklyn. He was an amazingly effective witness, and at the end of our time together I asked him to let me know the secret of his success. He was embarrassed by my question but finally said, "I just try to have two loves in my heart: for God and for the person who happens to be in front of me at any time." This simple but poignant statement has had a lasting effect on me.

I have come to realize that the summarized biblical statement "We are saved by the grace of God through faith in Jesus Christ" corrects an ancient—and still extant—belief that we must do something good in order to earn God's grace and love. It is not easy even for devout believers to realize that we do not have to work hard, be generous, obey the Ten Commandments, do good deeds, build Habitat houses, or forgive other people who harm us in order to be loved and accepted by our Creator. It is not what we do for God that is important but what we let God do for us. Faith brings about good works, but doing good things does not result in faith. However, having faith and returning the love of God to others should inspire us to do good things by emulating the example set on earth by Jesus Christ. We have to indicate our willingness to live a fruitful and happy life and then trust that we will be shown the way. As in the lives of the Ethredges, God often calls willing people to do good things, then qualifies them to do those things well.

One of the parables of Jesus that has been most difficult for me to understand is about the vineyard owner who hired some workers early in the morning and others throughout the day, including late in the afternoon. At sunset, he paid all of them the same amount he had promised the early workers, and those who had labored longest complained bitterly. The landowner replied, "'I am not being unfair to you, friend. Didn't you agree to work for a denarius? Take your pay and go. I want to give the one who was hired last the same as I gave you. Don't I have the right to do what I want with my own money?'" (Matthew 20:13–15). The lesson I have derived from this is that the vineyard owner represents God, who has the same love for everyone, no matter how much good work we do.

Another interesting but difficult parable of Jesus is about three servants who were given different sums by their master, who was going away on a long trip. The first was given five talents and the second two talents. They invested their money wisely and returned double the amount to their master when he came home. The third servant was given only one talent, which he buried and gave back to his returning boss, who sternly condemned him. I gather from this episode that we should use to the fullest degree whatever talents or opportunities we have been given, preferably for the benefit of others. In a more self-centered way, it has encouraged me to try new things, like seeking public office and even painting,

FAITH

writing books, composing poems, teaching Bible lessons, or woodworking.

Each Sunday at Maranatha I follow a general lesson outline from Smyth & Helwys Publishing Inc., which was established in 1991, at the same time as the Cooperative Baptist Fellowship. One of their suggested lesson series was about the well-known list of seven deadly sins, and although they are not listed as such in the Bible, each of them is covered quite thoroughly in separate verses. The named sins are lust, gluttony, greed, laziness, wrath, envy, and pride. When we studied this list, my class members and I agreed that the worst one of these is pride, which is most difficult to resist and leads to many immoral consequences. It is hard for any of us to claim that we have never exalted ourselves by acting as though we were superior to other persons. When we are excessively proud of ourselves, we tend to succumb to many of the other sins on the list as we forget our status as equal to all others in the eyes of God. There are many leaders of the Christian church today who practice superiority and exclusion, especially elevating the status of men to be superior to women. The Catholic hierarchy maintains that women are not qualified to be priests, deacons, or to hold other positions of authority in the Church, and Southern Baptists have similar rules that are even more repressive and discriminatory. This contradicts my interpretation of the life and teachings of Jesus, which exemplified equal status of all people.

There are a few biblical selections from St. Paul's letters

to the early churches that, taken out of historical context, seem to indicate his departure from Jesus' example of treating people as equals, and that show a bias against women by directing that they should be treated as second-class Christians. I do not maintain that these troubling scriptures are in error or that Paul disagreed with the teachings of Jesus, but it is necessary to assess the local circumstances within disputing early church congregations and interpret Paul's instructions to these "brothers and sisters" who were confused and disorderly. Paul is not mandating permanent or generic theological policies when he directs that women worship with their heads covered, keep their hair unbraided, dress modestly, and never adorn themselves or speak in a worship service. In a letter to his disciple Timothy, Paul even expressed a prohibition against women's teaching men, but we know, and Paul acknowledged, that Timothy himself was instructed in the Christian faith by his mother and grandmother. It is also difficult to understand how Paul's close friend Priscilla is revered for having been a teacher of Apollos, one of the great evangelists of that day, so that Apollos could more accurately explain that Jesus was indeed the long-awaited Messiah.

One of the frequently used biblical quotations by male chauvinists is "Wives, submit yourselves to your own husbands, as you do to the Lord. For the husband is the head of the wife, even as Christ is head of the church." However, they fail to include the incisive and challenging admonition that follows: "Husbands, love your wives, just as Christ loved the church and gave himself up for her. . . . In this same way, husbands ought to love their wives as their own bodies. He who loves his wife loves himself. . . . However, each one of you also must love his wife as he loves himself, and the wife must respect her husband" (Ephesians 5:22–33). What is called for in the text is not submission of women to men but equal submission of each to the other.

To resolve the apparent disharmony between Jesus and Paul, I have already referred to some of Paul's other remarks. In his letter to the Galatians, he stated, "You are all children of God through faith. . . . There is neither Jew nor Gentile, neither slave nor free, nor is there male and female; for you are all one in Christ Jesus." Also, in his letter to the Romans, Paul thanked twenty-eight outstanding leaders of the early churches, at least ten of whom were women: "I commend to you our sister Phoebe, a deacon of the church in Cenchreae. . . . Greet Priscilla and Aquila, my co-workers in Christ Jesus. . . . Greet Mary, who worked very hard for you. . . . Greet Andronicus and Junia, my fellow Jews who have been in prison with me. They are outstanding among the apostles, and they were in Christ before I was. . . . Greet Philologus, Julia, Nereus and his sister, and Olympas and all the Lord's people who are with them" (Romans 16:1–15). It is inconceivable to me that Paul would encourage and congratulate inspired women who were successful deacons, apostles, ministers, and saints and still be quoted by male chauvinists as a biblical source for excluding women from accepting God's call to serve others in the name of Christ. Paul has not separated himself from the lesson that Jesus taught: that women are to be treated equally in their right to serve God. Devout Christians can find scriptures to justify either side in this debate. The question is whether we evangelical believers in Christ want to abandon his example and exclude a vast array of potential female partners, who are equally devout and responding to God's call.

In modern times, Orthodox Jewish men thank God in their prayers for not being Gentiles, slaves, or women, and in the time of Jesus, there were several walls around the temple in Jerusalem that divided people in order of religious status: separating the high priest and other priests; priests and lay worshippers; men and women; Jews and Gentiles. Jesus attempted to break down walls between the Jewish leaders and the common people and between rich people and the poor, and he elevated the status of tax collectors, lepers, the blind and physically handicapped, Samaritans, and others who were despised or vilified. This commitment to equality before God was one of Jesus' most radical innovations in religion and in the society of his day. It seems to me that Jesus introduced for the first time the concept of caring primarily about the suffering or needs of others, not ourselves.

Recently, I asked my Bible class to list the items that now seem to be supported or condemned most enthusiastically within our various Christian denominations, and they quickly named abortion, homosexuality, prayer in public schools, use of public funds to support religious education, the ordination of women as priests, the inerrancy of the Bible, the priesthood of believers, the autonomy of local congregations, the glorification of pastors, and the breakdown of barriers between church and state. All these issues are important and worth debating, but none should become the basis of division or exclusion among believers.

When we brand people as enemies we can learn to derogate and hate them. Many years ago, I wrote a poem about how we quickly learn to despise our wartime enemies by referring to them as Huns, Wops, Japs, or Kooks. Jesus taught us not ever to exalt ourselves—and even to love our enemies.

I have not had serious doubts about my Christian faith since that time of taking Ruth's advice, and this confidence is something that is not easy for me to explain. My sustained belief may still be because of the remaining influence of my parents' unquestioning faith and because I have never had any further reason to distrust or reject my growing personal relationship with Jesus Christ and God. I have continued to study and teach the Bible, and more than forty years ago Rosalynn and I began to alternate reading aloud from the Scriptures or some other religious text each night. When we have been in different places, at least we knew we were considering the same ideas. I feel sure that our shared religious faith has helped us be reconciled after our inevitable disputes, and has provided an element of stability in our marriage.

I have continued to feel a need for something transcendent in my life on which I could always depend. I have wanted to have perpetual access to my Creator and to the teachings of Jesus, and I need to have something and someone through whom to explain the meaning of my life and who can provide guidance on how to live. My life is easier and more pleasant without having to make constant difficult choices and judgments on my own. When I utilize my human freedom to make multiple daily decisions, I have felt a need for guidance and a vision of some goal or framework within which to shape myself. I realize that none of us is either indispensable or useless, and that our value as human beings is a choice we make in our freedom. Having faith, I accept that any truth, scientific or otherwise, must be in harmony with my concept of God. Otherwise, how can I explain the origin of the universe, or the meaning of my life?

Another personal benefit that I derive from my faith—at least, most of the time—is a realization that it is my own fault if I feel lonely, alienated, unhappy, frustrated, inadequate, bereft of purpose, or afraid. This tends to prevent my blaming other people for my own problems. It is reassuring to realize also that all of us are created with all the talents and opportunities we need, in order to be completely successful in the eyes of God. We may doubt this if we are mentally deficient, lack an adequate education, or were raised or still live in abject poverty. In assessing our degree of success in life, most of us would consider things like financial income and security, number and loyalty of friends, quality of our home, public esteem, or a long life. Most Christians will realize that Jesus had none of these, but he was the epitome of success.

One episode that I remember tends to illustrate this point. I had a telephone call when I was governor from Dr. Norman Vincent Peale, who at that time was editor of *Guideposts* magazine, a frequent guest at the White House, and the author of *The Power of Positive Thinking,* which was on the *New York Times* bestseller list for more than three and a half years. He asked me to join him in speaking to an audience in Macon, Georgia, where about 7,500 people would come to witness a national Horatio Alger award being given to the congregation of a small church that had been "successful in spite of difficult circumstances." I was excited to be invited but had some trepidation about a potential comparison with one of the most famous speakers in the world. When we arrived in Macon a few weeks later, I learned that the church members were all mentally handicapped. I delivered my carefully prepared and rehearsed speech, Dr. Peale spoke eloquently as usual, and the final ceremony was for the church members to walk down the center aisle, light a huge candle, and receive the award. A middle-aged woman had this honor, was handed a lighted taper, and she and her fellow church members moved forward to the dais. Unfortunately, her hand was shaking badly, and she was unable to bring the flame in touch with the candle. The entire crowd was distressed, and we held our breath while she failed several times. She pushed the pastor's hand away when he tried to steady her elbow, she finally lit the candle, and the audience burst into sustained applause. I still remember how her face glowed with beauty and pure happiness, and I am certain that no one who was there will remember anything Dr. Peale or I had to say, or forget the inspiration we received as her shining face mirrored such a great success.

All my Christian achievements have been quite limited in scope and effect, except that while I was president I was given an opportunity to make a substantial contribution to the worldwide Christian Church. During 1978 I conducted secret long-distance discussions with Vice Premier Deng Xiaoping, who was the undisputed leader of the People's Republic of China. The United States and China had not had diplomatic relations for more than thirty years, while we had retained diplomatic ties with Taiwan after our military ally, Generalissimo Chiang Kai-shek, retreated there when his army was driven from the mainland by the forces of Mao Zedong. There was a powerful lobby in the United States that was dedicated to continuing our military and commercial ties with Taiwan, and after President Richard Nixon went to China and announced that there was only one China, the China we continued to recognize was not the Communist mainland but the small island of Taiwan. Deng and I negotiated for many months, and I never sent a message from the State Department because of the need to keep knowledge of the proceedings secret. All my dispatches to Beijing were transmitted directly from the White House. After the major disagreements were resolved, Deng and I

FAITH

were able to announce our decision in December of that year that reciprocal diplomatic recognition between the United States and the People's Republic of China would be effective at the beginning of the new year. Deng came to visit me that January, and we worked assiduously during his nine-day visit to conclude dozens of agreements that would consummate our new official relations.

Most people in America had been persuaded by the news media and statements of public officials that the "Red Chinese" were to be avoided and despised, but the tiny stature, sense of humor, and outgoing personality of Deng Xiaoping quickly changed public opinion. He made it clear in speeches and interviews that this new relationship would permit China to be much more deeply involved with the outside world, and that the people within China would also have a greatly expanded life. Far beyond what I imagined at the time, both of these expectations have been exceeded. I have been welcomed to China frequently since then, and am always treated like a hero.

During the formal White House banquet that Rosalynn and I hosted for our Chinese visitors, Deng leaned over and said softly, "Mr. President, you have helped to achieve great things for the Chinese people, and I wonder if there is anything we could do in China for you." After a few moments, I recalled that during my childhood our most revered heroes were Christian missionaries in China, especially a woman named Lottie Moon, and that under the Communist regime all missionaries had been expelled, and neither Bibles nor worship were permitted. I finally responded, "Yes, there are three things that I would like: for your government to let people worship freely, to own Bibles, and for our missionaries to return." He seemed taken aback and replied, "Well, I will have to think about this, and will let you know."

The next morning, Deng told me that he would grant two of my requests, but that no foreign missionaries would be permitted to come back into the country because they had acted like superiors and attempted to change Chinese cultural habits. When Rosalynn and I visited China in 1981, there was a new law that guaranteed freedom of worship, Bibles were plentiful, and overcrowded Christian churches were thriving. Some of the churches we attended in Shanghai were having to hold four services each Sunday to accommodate the large attendance. In 2010 the Pew Research Center's Forum on Religion and Public Life reported that there were more than 58 million Protestants in China, and in 2014 some leading experts on religion in China projected that by 2025 there would be more Protestant worshippers in China than in the United States. During our frequent trips to the country, Rosalynn and I have visited many churches and talked to their pastors, most of whom register their congregations with the government and some who refrain from doing so. Amity Press in Nanjing, China, is now the world's largest Bible publisher.

* * *

Neither my faith in Jesus Christ nor my faith in God has come to me originally or directly through the Bible, but studying the Scriptures helps explain and strengthen these relationships. Faith encompasses a real trusting of Jesus, and a continuing ability to find answers through him about my own life. Richard Niebuhr said that Christian faith always achieves "contemporaneousness with Christ." He goes on to explain that those who have this faith feel that we and Jesus are always living together, at the same time and in the same place, and that we are more closely connected to Jesus and other people of the past than we are with those who are now living in a distant place like Asia. The faith of Abraham is the same as the much later faith of Moses, the prophets, or Paul. I never have any experience without the assurance that Jesus is my companion, but I admit that I am not always aware of his presence unless something causes me to remember it. To me, Jesus Christ is not an object to be worshipped but a person and a constant companion. I pray in his name to the Father, and I seek through him to understand our present world and to better comprehend my own duties and responsibilities in dealing with daily life. I have no doubt that Jesus is living now, not simply that once upon a time Jesus existed. I look on him as the epitome of love, and of all that is good.

Of course, Christian faith has its origin in our belief in God, but it is aligned with the ideals and the example of the life of Jesus. Through him Christians hope to comprehend the mystery of God and his grace and seek to know and become obedient to God. To a Christian, faith is not dormant but causes us to learn more about our Creator and to develop and use our talents in an optimum way. I try to remember what I frequently teach: that the love and grace of God does not have to be earned; the message is not "Try harder and do better" but "Receive the gift with happiness, and show your gratitude by sharing God's love with others." Christians should be known by our love—and our laughter. I have used the word "grace" several times, and there is some understandable confusion when the Bible speaks of grace and mercy. A simple explanation that I like is that mercy is not getting the punishment we deserve, while grace is getting God's unbounded love that we don't deserve. I guess it is possible for someone to deny God's grace and love because of a complete lack of faith or because of an unpleasant event or an unanswered prayer request, but I believe this unfortunate person still retains the love of God, who is waiting for a more favorable response. After all, we must remember that all of us are given both life and the freedom to make our own decisions, even the rejection of belief that God exists.

In many ways, Rosalynn and I were devastated after my defeat for reelection as president in 1980. We had really wanted another four years in the White House and had many plans for ourselves and our nation. Now all these hopes were shattered, and at the age of fifty-six I was too young to consider retirement. Without seriously considering any other option, we decided to return to our home in Plains, but we still had no idea what to do. Our farms and warehouse business had been in a blind trust, and we learned from our trustee that we had suffered heavy financial losses while we were away, and were almost a million dollars in debt. It seemed that we might have to sell all our farmland to pay what we owed. After about three months, however, a large agricultural corporation (Archer Daniels Midland) decided to enter the peanut market, and they bought our warehouse and six others in the Southeast to give them an adequate supply of the crop. Back home, we resumed our role as active members of our local church, repaired our house and grounds, put a floor in the attic to store possessions accumulated during the past nine years of public service and campaigning, became reacquainted with our farms and woodlands, and settled our urgent business affairs. We also tried to inventory what we might have to invest in a productive future life, realizing that our experiences in Washington had given us unique insights into world affairs and familiarity with many foreign leaders that could be helpful. We would start by building the obligatory presidential library and museum, getting me a job for necessary family income, and writing our memoirs.

After a lot of prayer and discussion, we decided to develop The Carter Center, to be located alongside the presidential library in Atlanta. Rosalynn and I agreed on a few basic guidelines for our new Center to follow, including that it would be nonpartisan, not afraid to risk failure on projects that were worthwhile, eager to let local people take credit for any successes in their villages, and that it would avoid projects that would duplicate or compete with what others were doing well. This meant that if the World Bank, United Nations agencies, the U.S. government, or some university or nongovernmental organization was dealing effectively with a problem, we would devote ourselves to other issues. Almost by default, much of our overseas work has been in Latin America and Africa— regions that tend to be neglected by most governmental and social agencies.

We learned quickly that working as equals with needy people on common projects tended to forge almost instantaneous and binding ties, regardless of geographic separation or other differences. In the ghetto areas of great cities, on American Indian reservations, and in the villages of extremely poor countries like Chad, Haiti, Ethiopia, and Sudan, I have seen the emotional effect of sharing an opportunity for a better home, an increased yield of food grains, a clean water supply, or relief from a devastating disease. There is an instant and overwhelming melding of cultures, languages, and interests into a spirit of friendship and love.

Much more than when I was president, I now understand the potential benefits of working among some of the world's poorest people. Unfortunately, relatively little attention is given to these opportunities for our country to demonstrate world leadership by sharing any generous portion of our great wealth. For some reason, the words "foreign aid" have become dirty words, to be avoided by any candidate for public office.

* * *

Periodically, my Bible class and I study the life of Solomon, King David's son, to whom God offered any gift he wanted, as described in 1 Kings 3: "At Gibeon the Lord appeared to Solomon in a dream, and God said, 'Ask for whatever you want me to give you.'" After considering all his needs and desires, Solomon finally asked for wisdom, or "a diserning heart." After some discussion, we usually agree that each of us has a similar gift from God. We are given life, and complete freedom to make our own choices. It is this human freedom that imposes on us both responsibility and opportunity. We are not automatons but have unrestricted control over our own decisions after considering the circumstances at the time. We all decide for ourselves whether to be truthful, kind, generous, and loving, and we can show our gratitude to God by being good stewards of his creation. With each decision throughout life we shape our own character and destiny by making the basic choice: "This is the kind of person I want to be." Regardless of our wealth, education, or other blessings, each of us can decide whether we want to be kind or cruel, generous or selfish, humble or proud, truthful or a liar, peaceful or combative, and loving or hateful.

If we are doubtful about how we should act as a human, we have the perfect life of Jesus Christ that we can attempt to emulate. It makes our decisions easier when we have the faith and personal courage to act in this way, making the myriad choices and judgments that we face during our lifetimes. We learn the parameters or guidelines of a living faith from religious teaching and from personal experience—not from scientific theory or human laws. For instance, the importance of telling the truth has been deeply engrained in me, first by my father and then at the U.S. Naval Academy. Daddy always reserved his most severe disapproval for any of us children who made a false statement to him or my mother. At Annapolis, we midshipmen all knew that any revealed lie would be punished by instant dismissal.

I guess that most people are like me and have reluctant and uncontrollable doubts about people or things in which we want to have faith. One of the premises of Paul Tillich is that doubt is an integral facet of faith, implying a continual search and never a final answer. He also said, "Doubt is not the opposite of faith; it is one element of faith." I remember the father described in Mark 9, who wanted Jesus to cure his sick son but expressed some doubt about Jesus' ability to do so. Jesus replied that everything is possible for those who believe. The father exclaimed, "I do believe; help me overcome my unbelief!" I presume from the good result that his desire for faith was fulfilled, and at times I have made the same prayerful request, often with similar outcomes.

There were a number of times as president when I prayed that I would be able to succeed in reaching one of my political goals, and subsequently had serious doubts about my ability to do so. One of my most vivid memories of this kind was toward the end of my negotiations with President Sadat and Prime Minister Begin at Camp David. It was the thirteenth and final day, and we all thought we had failed in our effort to bring peace between Egypt and Israel. Begin would not accept my final drafted letter regarding the status of Jerusalem. My staff were already preparing a speech of regret and explanation for me to deliver to a joint session of Congress. Begin had asked for eight copies of a photograph of us three leaders, to be given to his grandchildren as mementos of our heroic but failed effort. My secretary, Susan Clough, had obtained the names of the children so I could personalize the photos, and I took them to Begin's cabin. He was sitting on the front porch, very distraught and nervous because the talks had finally broken down. I handed him the photographs, and he looked down and saw his granddaughter's name on the top one. He spoke it aloud, and then looked at each photograph individually, repeating the name of the grandchild I had written on it. His lips trembled, and tears welled up in his eyes. He asked me to step into his cabin, requesting that everyone else in the room leave. He was quiet, sober, and surprisingly friendly. Then he said that Jerusalem was so important that he could not accept my final letter.

When I found Sadat and told him what had happened, he was already dressed to go back to Washington. Then Begin called and said, "I have decided to accept the letter you have drafted on Jerusalem." A short time later we were on the way to Washington, all three of us talking to Presidents Nixon and Ford to tell them that we would have peace in the future.

One of the most severe tests of faith in my own survival began in July 2015, when I was in Guyana leading a team from The Carter Center in monitoring one of that country's hotly contested elections. I developed a terrible cold, but felt even worse than I expected. After examining me, a young doctor from Johns Hopkins recommended that I return home. I refused to comply with her recommendation, so she sent me to a local hospital in Georgetown, where a Cuban doctor confirmed and emphasized her recommendation. His prevailing argument was that I was likely to contaminate any Guyanese people whom I would contact. I returned to Atlanta, and the physicians at Emory Hospital determined with MRI scans that I had a cancerous place in my liver, which a surgeon removed. After I recovered from the surgery and Rosalynn and I were driving back to my home in Plains a few days later, I had a telephone call from an oncologist who informed me that a later MRI scan had revealed several cancer spots in my brain, and that the problems were caused by melanoma (skin cancer) that had metastasized. My father and my three siblings had all died of pancreatic cancer, three of them at a relatively young age, so we thought that I had only a few weeks to live. Rosalynn and I began making plans for my death and notified the members of our family and key staff at The Carter Center. I was surprised and pleased to discover that I was not afraid, but overwhelmingly grateful for my long and good life while sad to be leaving the people I loved.

I had found the ability to face the uncertainty of extended life with equanimity, and commitment to a higher calling was my best source of strength. It is difficult to explain, but I found this sense of inevitability and acceptance to be most similar to my feelings as a young submarine officer, when everyone who served in the military had to accommodate the prospect of potential death. We had a remarkable sense of liberation when we left our home port for a wartime cruise. The multitude of life's routine responsibilities and worries could be forgotten, with our concerns limited to those duties within the narrow confines of the submarine hull. Our written monthly reports concerning personnel and equipment were in abeyance until we returned, and even the cherished duties of a husband and father were left behind. I would be with seventy-one other men for a preordained time and, of necessity, I had faith in the abilities and steadfastness of my fellow crewmen. The duties were onerous but, except for unforeseen crises within the ship, they were routine and predictable. The simplicity of this life was surprisingly satisfying. I dealt with potential concerns, even the possibility of tragedy, by focusing on my immediate duties, realizing that all results could not be under my control. On the ship, we all knew that a few dozen special people shared a close bond, each depending on all the others.

Interested in my cancer, the news media inundated my staff with questions, so I decided to hold a news conference and answer any questions that might be forthcoming. The interrogation lasted more than an hour, and oncologist Walter Curran was present to answer medical questions after I left. The next day the spots in my brain were treated with radiation, and I learned about a new and experimental treatment for melanoma called pembrolizumab (Keytruda), which might be successful in enhancing my autoimmune system to fight cancer. However, in some preliminary tests, it had been found to have a beneficial effect in only about 35 percent of cases. I began receiving the first of eight infusion treatments, and the doctors soon reported that I was fortunate in that my body was responding favorably. When I returned home to Plains, the streets and front yards were covered with political-type campaign signs saying, "JIMMY CARTER FOR CANCER SURVIVOR." I completed the pembrolizumab treatments and have continued to have regular MRI scans of my body and brain, so far with favorable results. We have reduced our overseas travel schedule, but Rosalynn and I still exercise regularly, continue general management of Carter Center affairs, and respond to correspondence, and I teach my Bible lessons in Plains and classes at Emory University in Atlanta.

About a year later, when Rosalynn and I passed the seventieth year of our marriage, we had a lot of questions about whether we had any secrets to a successful partnership. Our brief reply was that we have learned to give each other plenty of space to pursue our individual interests, try to maintain easy communication, and resolve our frequent differences before going to sleep at night. It is not usually the big arguments that matter, but the year-by-year, dozen-times-a-day little things that can destroy a marriage or make it successful. In almost every close relationship, times arise when the husband and wife look on the same event with different perspectives. If it is possible to discuss contrary views with honesty and mutual respect—a big if—many problems can be avoided. We have to be willing to forgive, because mistakes are inevitable. There is going to be anger and even, at times, deliberately hurtful words, so understanding and flexibility are required. And it is crucial during times of crisis to maintain an unshakable foundation of permanence. For Rosalynn and me, the solemn marriage vows have been a powerful stabilizing force, largely because we consider these pledges to be inviolate. In addition to what we learn about religion and life by reading together, there is an element of self-discipline about this ritual that is beneficial.

If we examine the basic elements of a marriage, we see that the same things apply in our relationship with Christ: love, forgiveness, loyalty, flexibility, the admission of mistakes, looking inward, and the ability to ask, "What is there about my life that is not acceptable to you?"—along with a willingness to change. Each Christian has, in effect, gone through a marriage vow with Jesus, and it is a form of adultery to violate this pledge by putting anything above the relationship with him. Being faithful to God has helped me to strengthen commitments within my family, in military service, and in political office. It has been good for me to remember that it was "before God" that I took all these oaths to fulfill obligations to the best of my ability.

Religious faith is not something that can be explained, any more easily than love. I could not have understood love before I fell in love with Rosalynn. The close and trusting relationship with my parents and sisters was in no way equivalent to how I came to feel about her. There was total confidence, ease of communication, and mutual dependency that was unprecedented. I could not describe the meaning of love to another person any better than before, but for the first time I understood what loving could mean to a human being. I did not do anything to make myself love her; it just happened as one of my life's blessings. It is the same with my Christian faith.

People in my Bible class often ask what it means to be a Christian. My best explanation is that a Christian is a person professing Jesus Christ as a personal savior, and striving to have the human qualities demonstrated by Jesus. The indefinable character of God can be envisioned only through the mixture of these apparently incompatible characteristics in the life of Jesus. He was both God and man, all-powerful but gentle and loving, all-knowing, compassionate, suffering, despised, burdened with the sin of others, abandoned by his followers, publicly executed but resurrected, and now worshipped by billions of believers throughout the world. Personal faith in Christ and a special reverence for him help us comprehend

God's transcendent love. At the same time, I have never found anything in the strictly human life of Jesus that was not admirable and inspirational. Whether or not a doubtful person can accept Jesus' divinity, there is in him a model of human existence to be studied and emulated. Sometimes I remind my class members that one of the definitions of a Christian might be a "little Christ," and we all agree that this is a personally embarrassing claim to make. This reminds us that we assume the same responsibility for our own behavior when we say, "I am a Christian." One of the facets of this declaration is that we accept the fact that with the willing self-sacrifice of Jesus on the cross, our faith in him can let him bear the punishment for all our sins. I used to accept this belief quite casually until I was teaching its meaning to my class. It became much more difficult and momentous to me when I envisioned my young daughter having to accept the punishment for all my sins. If it were Amy instead of Jesus, I would be much more averse to criticizing others, making an incorrect statement, ignoring a needy person, or failing in my other Christian duties.

Jesus made a brief statement to a leading Pharisee that describes the foundation of Christianity: "For God so loved the world that he gave his only son, that whoever believes in him shall not perish but will have eternal life. For God did not send his son into the world to condemn the world, but to save the world through him" (John 3:16–17). The entire statement is profoundly important, but the first six words, often overlooked, show God's equal and universal love for everyone.

Jesus' dramatic and often delightful experiences are always inspirational, and they offer examples of how to deal with our opportunities, afflictions, and concerns in a reassuring and joyful way. They give us priorities or standards for living. Almost any of our most exalted ideals can be understood, clarified, and expanded by what Jesus said and did. Jesus' teachings can help to keep us at peace with both our Creator and our neighbors. All of this can be gratifying and valuable, regardless of our public profession of faith. One common goal in life is happiness, and it is the keeping of God's commandments that provides us with a real opportunity to experience this pleasure. The Scriptures say, "If you keep my commandments, you will remain in my love. . . . I have told you this so that my joy may be in you and that your joy may be complete" (John 15:10, 11). When was the last time we felt almost totally at ease within ourselves? Through religious faith we are promised peace, even when we are worried or filled with fear: "Peace I leave with you; my peace I give you. . . . Do not let your hearts be troubled and do not be afraid" (John 14:27). And we are promised "the peace of God, which transcends all understanding" in our hearts and minds (Philippians 4:7). We are offered these blessings through faith.

Looking perhaps at the distant future, I have faith that God is slowly bending eternity toward redemption, and that someday, as a result of evolutionary progress, moral perfection based on love as expressed by Jesus Christ will prevail.

SIX

Challenges to Faith

The sad duty of politics is to establish justice
in a sinful world. —Reinhold Niebuhr

The ultimate test of a moral society is the kind of world
that it leaves to its children. —Dietrich Bonhoeffer

Racism is man's gravest threat to man—
the maximum hatred for a minimum of
reason. —Abraham Joshua Heschel

It is likely that many people have been discouraged and frustrated in every historical era, with some always believing that "these are the most troubling and disappointing of times." I have lived through two such periods in my own life: the Great Depression and World War II. I was five years old when the first of these global tragedies began with the stock market crash of 1929 in the United States, when the world's total income fell by an estimated 15 percent and at least one-fourth of the workers in the United States were unemployed. The dirt road in front of our house, U.S. Highway 280, ran from Savannah on the east coast to Columbus, and then divided to go south through Montgomery and on to Los Angeles and north through Birmingham to San Francisco. Our family had a vivid reminder of the extent of this American economic tragedy as dozens of "hoboes" walked by our home each day, most of them workers who had lost their jobs in Northern states and had come south to stay warm during the cold months and to seek food or especially any kind of job. Many of the family groups included women and children. Other transients passed our house riding in empty boxcars on the trains of the Seaboard Air Line Railroad, whose owners broke their normal rules to accommodate the plight of so many fellow citizens who needed a train ride. My mother was especially gracious to those who came to our door for help.

Our family continued to enjoy a comfortable home, but we shared the general economic burden, as the prices of our crops and livestock fell about 60 percent. Land also became very cheap. I remember when my father refused a wealthy city quail hunter's offer of the price of a two-hundred-acre farm for one of our best bird dogs. My parents and our neighbors were economically depressed, but our local school was still a source of pride and the dozen or so churches in the Plains community of five hundred people were filled with faithful worshippers. My impression was that our religious faith and gracious dependence on one another reached a high point.

The United States was making a strong economic recovery when World War II began, but the adverse impact of the

Great Depression years was still being felt in many countries. Our naval forces in Pearl Harbor, Hawaii, were attacked on December 7, 1941, and the United States entered the war as an active participant. I was a new high school graduate, and my only close family member affected by the new conflict was my hero and favorite uncle, Tom Gordy. He was taken prisoner when Japanese forces overran the island of Guam just three days after the Pearl Harbor attack. Uncle Tom was one of the radiomen stationed on the island to help provide communication among the widely dispersed ships and naval bases of the Pacific Fleet, and he and his fellow navy men had been ordered not to resist the invasion in order to prevent the killing of natives on the island. Tom's wife and their three children came to live on a farm adjacent to ours. The next year I enrolled in the Naval Reserve Officers' Training Corps at Georgia Tech, and remained in the U.S. Navy for the next eleven years, until October 1953. My last sea duty as an officer in the Pacific Ocean was on a submarine during the Korean War.

The next major military conflict for the United States was the Vietnam War, in which our oldest son, Jack, left college and volunteered to serve. Our country was involved in this conflict for about fifteen years (1960–1975), and it was a time when American public opinion about the war became increasingly divided. I remember that Jack was sometimes reluctant to wear his naval uniform when he was back in America on leave, because of the derision and animosity shown to our servicemen. There were many misleading statements made in

Washington concerning the conduct of the war, the battle areas being contested, the casualties on both sides, and prospects for victory, and the faith of our citizens in top public officials was badly shaken. Our family members were strong supporters of President Lyndon Johnson, and I was shocked and disappointed when he announced on television that he would not be a candidate for reelection—probably because of negative public opinion about the war.

There was a relative lull in serious combat involving the United States after Vietnam, until the terrorist attacks on the World Trade Center and the Pentagon on September 11, 2001. As a response, the U.S. government overreacted to the threat of further acts of terrorism by clamping down on individual rights of our own citizens, permitting the torture of prisoners, incarcerating accused people without trial or even clear charges against them, and disavowing Geneva Conventions restraints and other international agreements about the treatment of captives. We also initiated the seemingly never-ending wars in Iraq and Afghanistan.

Unlike some people of faith, I have never believed that pacifism is a necessary element of Christianity. This is a decision I made when I joined the navy in 1942. I knew there would be times during the war when I might have to take human life—or lose my own—in defense of my country. Had my religious faith been the same as what the Quakers, Amish, Mennonites, and some others espouse, I would have become a conscientious objector rather than serve in the military. I might also never have sought high public office, since this could have required me, as president, to send others to their deaths. But pacifism was not my choice.

Even before my inauguration as president, I became thoroughly briefed about our military forces, and I consulted then and throughout my term with wise and knowledgeable people who shared my cautious approach to the use of our military power. My primary commitment was to protect America's interests while living peacefully with others who had contrary concerns. However, if peacekeeping efforts failed, as happened before the two World Wars, then I was prepared to use force if necessary. During the Cold War, I felt that mutual foreknowledge of our mighty response capability was the greatest deterrence to an enemy attack and the global destructiveness of a third world war, perhaps including the use of nuclear weapons. Thus, although the life-and-death power I held as commander in chief was sobering, I was and am convinced of the moral rightness of maintaining America's military strength.

I was fortunate to avoid armed conflict as president, and I have opposed most of the subsequent military engagements of our country. In March 2003, as we prepared for war in Iraq, I wrote an op-ed entitled "Just War—or a Just War?" The text included these words:

Profound changes have been taking place in American foreign policy, reversing consistent bipartisan commitments that for more than two centuries have earned our nation greatness. These commitments have been predicated on basic religious principles, respect for international law, and alliances that resulted in wise decisions and mutual restraint. Our apparent determination to launch a war against Iraq, without international support, is a violation of these premises.

As a Christian and as a president who was severely provoked by international crises, I became thoroughly familiar with the principles of a just war, and it is clear that a substantially unilateral attack on Iraq does not meet these standards. This is an almost universal conviction of religious leaders, with the most notable exception of a few spokesmen of the Southern Baptist Convention who are greatly influenced by their commitment to Israel based on eschatological, or final days, theology.

For a war to be just, it must meet several clearly defined criteria.

The war can be waged only as a last resort, with all nonviolent options exhausted. In the case of Iraq, it is obvious that clear alternatives to war exist. These options—previously proposed by our own leaders and approved by the United Nations—were outlined again by the Security Council on Friday. But now, with our own national security not directly threatened and despite the overwhelming opposition of most people and governments in the world, the United States seems determined to carry out military and diplomatic action that is almost unprecedented in the history of civilized nations. The first stage of our widely publicized war plan is to launch 3,000 bombs and missiles on a relatively defenseless Iraqi population within the first few hours of an invasion, with the purpose of so damaging and demoralizing the people that they will change their obnoxious leader, who will most likely be hidden and safe during the bombardment.

The war's weapons must discriminate between combatants and noncombatants. Extensive aerial bombardment, even with precise accuracy, inevitably results in "collateral damage." Gen. Tommy R. Franks, commander of American forces in the Persian Gulf, has expressed concern about many of the military targets being near hospitals, schools, mosques and private homes.

Its violence must be proportional to the injury we have suffered. Despite Saddam Hussein's other serious crimes, American efforts to tie Iraq to the 9/11 terrorist attacks have been unconvincing.

The attackers must have legitimate authority sanctioned by the society they profess to represent. The unanimous vote of approval in the Security Council to eliminate Iraq's weapons of mass destruction can still be honored, but our announced goals are now to achieve regime change and to establish a Pax Americana in the region, perhaps occupying the ethnically divided country for as long as a decade. For these objectives, we do not have international authority. Other members of the Security Council have so far resisted the enormous economic and political influence that is being exerted from Washington, and we are faced with the possibility of either a failure to get the necessary votes or else a veto from Russia, France and China. Although Turkey may still be enticed into helping us by enormous financial rewards and partial future control of the Kurds and oil in northern Iraq, its democratic Parliament has at least added its voice to the worldwide expressions of concern.

The peace it establishes must be a clear improvement over what exists. Although there are visions of peace and democracy in Iraq, it is quite possible that the aftermath of a military invasion will destabilize the region and prompt terrorists to further jeopardize our security at home. Also, by defying overwhelming world opposition, the United States will undermine the United Nations as a viable institution for world peace.

What about America's world standing if we don't go to war after such a great deployment of military forces in the region? The heartfelt sympathy and friendship offered to America after the 9/11 attacks, even from formerly antagonistic regimes, has been largely dissipated; increasingly unilateral and domineering policies have brought international trust in our country to its lowest level in memory. American stature will surely decline further if we launch a war in clear defiance of the United

Nations. But to use the presence and threat of our military power to force Iraq's compliance with all United Nations resolutions—with war as a final option—will enhance our status as a champion of peace and justice.

In my 2005 book *Our Endangered Values: America's Moral Crisis,* I deplored these and other recent developments. I pointed out that "with the most diverse and innovative population on earth, we have learned the value of providing our citizens with accurate information, treating dissenting voices and beliefs with respect, and accommodating free and open debate on controversial issues. Most of our political leaders have extolled state and local autonomy, attempted to control deficit spending, avoided foreign adventurism, minimized long-term peacekeeping commitments, preserved the separation of church and state, and protected civil liberties and personal privacy. All of these historic commitments are now being challenged."

In that book, I also covered a number of controversial subjects that were—and still are—dividing our people, including abortion, the death penalty, proliferation of guns, science versus religion, women's rights, the separation of religion and politics, homosexuality, America's foreign policy and our global image, civil liberties, the threat of terrorism, nuclear proliferation, the choice between peace and almost continual war, environmental degradation, and equity between the rich and poor. In scanning the text recently, I notice that I used the word "faith" more than fifty times, mostly referring to my own or other people's beliefs, but also to "good faith diplomacy" and to our sometimes waning faith in freedom, democracy, justice, equality as citizens, and other basic human rights.

One of the most troubling political developments in recent years has been the extreme polarization of Americans and the virtual elimination from our national Congress of moderate leaders who are willing to compromise in order to evolve laws or even to be civil to one another. The two most important causes of this growing problem are the massive influx of money into political campaigns and the extreme gerrymandering of congressional districts when either Democrats or Republicans gain complete control of a state government. These factors tend to concentrate political influence in an ever-smaller group of citizens who are wealthier and more powerful, and they become the ones who gain most from new laws.

The United States has been an undisputed global superpower since World War II, with the dominant economy, military force, and cultural influence, but this era of preeminence is almost inevitably coming to a close as the relative influence of Russia, China, India, and other countries increases. An exceptionally strong Chinese leader, Xi Jinping, has, in effect, verbally challenged the United States with a claim of China's being the future global power, and his country is already expected to become the world's economic leader in the predictable future—primarily because of avoiding military engagements and having a single dominant Communist regime.

With world leadership, our country has chosen to become

involved in a growing number of disputes and military conflicts involving other countries, gaining a reputation among many people as the world's foremost belligerent. As early as 1953, President Dwight Eisenhower had worried about the direction that the United States and other nations were taking: "Every gun that is made, every warship launched, every rocket fired signifies, in the final sense, a theft from those who hunger and are not fed, those who are cold and are not clothed. This world in arms is not spending money alone. It is spending the sweat of its laborers, the genius of its scientists, the hopes of its children." When he left office in 1961, he warned: "In the councils of government, we must guard against the acquisition of unwarranted influence, whether sought or unsought, by the military-industrial complex. The potential for the disastrous rise of misplaced power exists and will persist." I share Eisenhower's concern, but this is a role that cannot be blamed just on the "military industrial complex," because our almost constant involvement in war has been approved and actively supported by many of our own citizens. There is a prevailing feeling that we Americans have a duty to act as a global policeman and that our armed intercessions are justified if they are designed to support a potential move toward our form of democratic government.

I remember that Deng Xiaoping asked for a private meeting with me when he was visiting Washington in January 1979, and he informed me that China was planning an invasion of Vietnam within the next few days. I objected, saying that this would not be good as an apparent result of our just-announced move to normalize diplomatic relations. He promised that the intrusion across the border would not be sustained, and within two months the invading Chinese forces had withdrawn. Since then, for about four decades, China has refrained from involving its military forces in war and has concentrated on economic progress, such as dramatically reducing the poverty rate, investing in more than fourteen thousand miles of rail lines with speeds above 250 miles per hour, building modern highways and bridges, founding new universities, and addressing other elements of its basic infrastructure.

In sharp contrast, the United States is neglecting its basic domestic needs. In August 2017, the World Bank found that among the fifty largest nations assessed, "The United States is forecast [by 2040] to have the largest infrastructure investment gap—the difference between investment needs and current trends in investment—of $3.8 trillion." One of the obvious causes of this growing domestic crisis is explained in an October 2017 report in *The New York Times,* which revealed that there were 240,000 American troops openly stationed in at least 172 foreign countries, plus more than 37,000 others in places militarily classified as secret. It is estimated that the total cost of the wars in Iraq and Afghanistan will be between $4 and $6 trillion. In comparison, our total proposed federal budget for 2017 was about $4.2 trillion, and our national debt now exceeds $20.5 trillion.

Our sustained use of force around the world, employing

airstrikes on targets in Syria, Afghanistan, Iraq, and Yemen, and drone strikes in several other countries, often results in high civilian casualties, which contradicts our claim to be a peaceful nation devoted to human rights. In none of these cases did we first exhaust the opportunities for peaceful resolution of the dispute, or apply the criteria of a "just war." The President of the United States is now given almost unilateral authority for such foreign military engagements, and the U.S. Congress is inclined to reject any offer from an incumbent president to share this responsibility. This massive involvement of our military forces overseas is one of the reasons that our general reputation suffers and intense hatred and violent attacks on us and our allies are sometimes engendered.

Even the long-lasting and unfocused imposition of sanctions or embargoes can be overdone. In my visits to targeted countries, I have seen how this strategy can be cruel to innocent people who have no influence on international disputes and are already suffering under dictatorships. Unless narrowly concentrated on domineering political leaders, economic punishment of unsavory regimes is most often ineffective and can be counterproductive. In Cuba, where the news media are controlled by the government, most people are convinced that their economic plight is caused by the United States and not their Communist system, and that they are being defended by the actions of their Communist leaders, who are therefore strengthened in power. I have visited the homes of both Castro brothers and some of the regime's other top officials, and it is obvious that their living conditions have not suffered because of the embargo. Many Cuban families are deprived of sustainable incomes, certain foods, cellphones, Internet access, and basic freedoms, but at least they have access to a good education and health care, and they live in a tropical environment where the soil is productive and where some fortunate families may have trees that bear bananas and other fruit. In addition, Cubans receive about $2 billion annually in remittances from friends and relatives in the United States.

The situation is more tragic in North Korea, where none of these advantages exist. The U.S. embargo, imposed sixty-eight years ago at the start of the Korean War, has been more strictly enforced, with every effort made to restrict or damage North Korea's economy. During my visits to Pyongyang, I have had extensive discussions with government officials and with forceful female leaders, who emphasized the plight of people who were starving. The United Nations's World Food Program estimates that at least 600 grams of cereal per day is needed for a "survival ration" and that the daily food distribution in North Korea has at times been as low as 128 grams. The last U.S. congressional staffers who were permitted to visit the country reported a range of 300,000 to 800,000 people dying each year from starvation.

In 2001, The Carter Center arranged for North Korean agricultural leaders to go to Mexico to learn how to increase production of potatoes and other indigenous crops, and the U.S. annual contribution of grain rose to 695,000 tons in the late 1990s during a brief period of U.S.–North Korean reconciliation. However, the contribution was reduced substantially under President George W. Bush and then terminated completely by President Obama in 2010. I visited the State Department then and was told that the main problem was North Korea's refusal to permit any supervision of food deliveries.

In 2011, I returned to North Korea, accompanied by former president of Finland Martti Ahtisaari, former president of Ireland Mary Robinson, and former prime minister of Norway Gro Brundtland, a physician who was also director of the World Health Organization. We stopped first in Beijing for briefings from U.N. World Food Program officials, who told us there were no restraints on monitoring of food deliveries to families in North Korea. They followed us to Pyongyang and accompanied us, free of government supervision, to rural areas where tiny food allotments were being distributed to families. The government gave us an official guarantee that all such food deliveries could be monitored by the United States and other donors. I reported this when I returned to Washington, with the assessment that one-third of North Korean children were malnourished and stunted in their growth and that daily food intake for an active man was between 700 and 1400 calories per person, compared with a recommended American equivalent being 2000 to 3000 calories. Our government took no action.

There is no excuse for oppression of citizens by dictatorial regimes like those in Cuba or North Korea, but the degree of harsh treatment depends at least partially on the dissatisfaction of the citizens. Starving people are more inclined to demand relief from their plight, protest, and be punished or executed. As in Cuba, the political elite in North Korea do not suffer, and the leaders' all-pervasive propaganda places the blame for their deprivation on the United States, not themselves. The primary objective of dictators is to stay in office, and we help them achieve this goal by punishing their already suffering subjects and letting the dictators claim to be saviors. When nonmilitary pressure on a government is considered necessary, economic sanctions should be focused on travel, foreign bank accounts, and other special privileges of government officials who make decisions, not on destroying the economy that determines the living conditions of oppressed people.

Throughout the world, the increasing disparity in wealth has long been troubling. As the new millennium approached in December 1999, I was invited to make two speeches to large and influential audiences, with the requested topic being "What is the greatest challenge facing the world in 2000?" In Taipei, Taiwan, and Oslo, Norway, I proposed that the answer to this question was the growing disparity in income, both within countries and between the richest and poorest nations, and I emphasized how rapidly the change was occurring. This trend has accelerated even more since that time, so that, in 2017, the eight richest people in the world (six of them

Americans) had as much net worth as the poorest half of the world's population—about 3.7 billion people. This trend is much the same within the United States and many other individual countries. Among Americans now, the richest 1 percent have about 40 percent of the total wealth, and leading economists report that, during the first four years after the 2009 economic recovery began, 95 percent of economic gains went to the wealthiest 1 percent. With politicians at all levels becoming increasingly obligated to wealthy contributors, our country is tending to change from a democracy into an oligarchy.

The unwarranted influence of a powerful lobby is also seen vividly in the proliferation of guns in the United States. The manufacture, transfer, and possession of nineteen specific semiautomatic assault weapons—including AK-47s, AR-15s, and Uzis—was formerly prohibited, but in 2004 the National Rifle Association (NRA) prevailed and Congress lifted the ban. These weapons are not used for hunting but only for killing other humans. The demand for assault weapons does not come from hunters, homeowners, or outdoorsmen but from gun manufacturers. I have owned and used weapons since I was big enough to carry one, and now own a handgun, four shotguns, and two rifles. I use them carefully, for harvesting game from our woods and fields and during an occasional foray to hunt with my family and friends in other places. But many of us who participate in outdoor sports are dismayed by some of the more extreme policies of the NRA and by the timidity of public officials who yield to their unreasonable demands. Heavily influenced and supported by the firearms industry, its primary client, the NRA has been able to mislead many gullible people into believing that all weapons are going to be taken away from us, and that homeowners will be deprived of the right to protect ourselves and our families. There are no real threats to our "right to bear arms," as guaranteed by the U.S. Constitution.

In addition to assault weapons, the gun lobby protects the ability of criminals and gang members to use ammunition that can penetrate protective clothing worn by police officers on duty and assures that a known or suspected terrorist is not barred from buying or owning a firearm—including an assault weapon. What are the results of this profligate ownership and use of guns designed to kill people? According to the Centers for Disease Control and Prevention (now prohibited by Congress from studying this issue), in 2016, there were more than 38,000 gun deaths in the United States, or about fifty-five times higher than the United Kingdom and ninety-six times more than Japan. About 23,000 of the 38,000 gun deaths were by suicide. The Children's Defense Fund reported that American children are sixteen times more likely to be killed with a gun than those in other developed countries. The NRA, the firearms industry, and compliant politicians should reassess their policies concerning gun safety and accountability. The two most effective legislative requirements that could address mass attacks and individual gun deaths are to outlaw military-type assault weapons and to require reasonable and universal background checks on purchasers of guns.

The scientific community knows that climate change is real, and that it is caused by human activity. It is already evident that global warming is causing devastating harm throughout the world. Further, the scientists tell us that if we do not act boldly to address the crisis, our planet will see more drought, more floods—the recent devastations by Hurricanes Harvey, Irma, and Maria are good examples—more extreme weather disturbances, more warming and acidification of the oceans, faster-rising sea levels, and, because of mass migrations, there will be more threats to global stability and security. Compliance by all nations with the Paris Accord would be helpful.

Another of our unmet challenges is that there are more than 2.2 million Americans now in prison—most of them for nonviolent crimes. This is the highest level of incarceration in the world. Among the busiest construction industries in many states are those that are building more jail cells, and job opportunities for prison guards have skyrocketed. In Georgia, our "two strikes and you're out" law will help to keep this punitive industry flourishing. Our country also stands almost alone in the world in our fascination with the death penalty, and our few remaining companions are regimes with a known lack of respect for basic human rights. The top countries in executions are China, Iran, Saudi Arabia, Iraq, Pakistan, Egypt, and the

United States. In fact, our nation is the only one that has refused to ratify the international Convention on the Rights of the Child, primarily because it prohibits execution for crimes committed by children. Since 1990 only eight countries other than the United States had executed people for crimes they committed as juveniles. Belatedly, in March 2005 the U.S. Supreme Court voted five to four to outlaw juvenile executions—a decision strongly condemned by many conservative Christians. It seems somewhat illogical to say: "You have violated God's commandment: 'Thou shalt not kill,' so therefore I will kill you." Fortunately, according to a Gallup poll, that is the philosophy of a dwindling number, but it's still 55 percent of Americans. In 1972, the Supreme Court ruled that capital punishment, as it was then administered, was "cruel and unusual" and therefore unconstitutional. In July 1976, however, the court overturned its previous ruling, imposed some restraints, and capital punishment was reinstated. I've always considered myself fortunate that while I was governor and president there was just one execution under my jurisdiction.

Almost all the occurrences and trends I've just described have been existing for twenty years or more, but some of them have been exacerbated as a result of the 2016 presidential election. The trend toward control of our democratic system of government by a small group of powerful and wealthy citizens and corporations was enhanced and solidified, false and illogical political claims have been rampant, ad hominem attacks on political opponents became normal and accepted, and serious allegations are being investigated about direct Russian involvement and interference in the electoral process. Candidates used social media (Facebook and Twitter) so they could focus false or misleading messages on specific individuals or targeted groups. "Alternative facts" became more common, and exposed lying more acceptable and forgivable. Our faith in the integrity and competence of government officials, our democracy, basic principles of justice, the truth, in fellow citizens, and in ourselves has been further shaken. Much of the international respect and admiration that our nation enjoyed for many decades is being dissipated. Irresponsible and uncontrollable public statements and tweets on social media by the president have brought us closer to our two foremost global threats: atmospheric warming and a possible nuclear war. There has been a further increase in racial tension and Islamophobia, immigrants are more uncertain about their status, and "fake news" is more deliberately and widely promulgated.

Most of these concerns are about legal decisions and actions by government officials, but it surprised my religion and theology students at Emory University when I said that most church members are more self-satisfied, more committed to the status quo, and more excluding of dissimilar people than are the political officeholders I have known. In considering these issues, many congregations are more like spectators than participants, usually waiting for an aggressive pastor or professional staff to inspire any corrective programs in their local communities. Of necessity, officeholders are involved in addressing all kinds of social needs, and in the political world at election time there is an inherent and unavoidable mechanism for public assessment of performance against expectations, a degree of rivalry in dealing with human problems in the most dedicated and effective manner, and the threat of removal from office for those who are seen to fail. Whether campaigning or serving in office, politicians cannot avoid the most difficult and controversial subjects. They are the ones on whom the news media focus and of whom judgments will be made—if they contravene the preferences of their constituents. Our governments are obviously fallible, and they deserve criticism for many defects and failures; in a democracy, free elections are supposed to correct errors and defects. It is well known that in politics moral standards are often ignored or circumvented, there are embarrassing revelations of malfeasance among officeholders, and some of them have been convicted of crimes, but some of the same problems afflict the religious world.

When I was serving on a county school board, in the Georgia senate, in the governor's office, and in the White House, I spent a major portion of my time exploring how I might resolve the most difficult issues. How could I join with others in helping to feed the hungry, cloth the naked, provide homes for the homeless, educate the illiterate, eliminate the stigma of poverty or racial discrimination, make peace and resolve differences between people, prevent crime, rehabilitate prisoners, and ensure justice? These were not just occasional concerns but constant preoccupations for me and for most others who served in political office. I admit that our public officials often fail to meet these criteria, but despite some wonderful exceptions, the same degree of commitment and willingness to address the problems of society is relatively rare in our religious congregations. I have been a member of some good churches, at home in Plains and near where we lived in Atlanta and Washington. Our men's classes have included some of the finest and most dedicated community leaders, and we have been proud in the practice of our Christian faith. It was common for us, as Thanksgiving or Christmas approached, to do something especially benevolent for the poor people near our place of worship. After we had taken up a nice collection, a frequent question was "Why don't we call the welfare office and get the names and addresses of some poor families, so we can take them what they need for a nice holiday meal?" But this was usually just a special seasonal interest in the needy, not one that prevailed throughout the year.

It is reassuring to realize that the highest goals of government are not incompatible with the secular ideals of religion. In *Reinhold Niebuhr on Politics,* the theologian wrote, "To establish justice in a sinful world is the whole sad duty of the political order. There has never been justice without law; and all laws are the stabilization of certain social equilibria, brought about by pressures and counter-pressures in society, and expressed in the structures of government." Niebuhr's obvious point is that the highest possible goal of a government or a society is to treat people fairly, to protect their safety, to guarantee their individual rights, to guard against discrimination, and to resolve disagreements peacefully. Most of us would agree that these goals are common to church and state. Given the pluralism in America today, I have grown fonder of the terms "religion and government" than "church and state," though I know the latter still communicates the basic ideas. However, any government, even the most benevolent, has inherent limitations. The best it can do is strive to establish a society that enhances freedom, equality, and justice.

There are deeper religious values, such as humility, atonement, forgiveness, compassion, and love, that transcend what a government can achieve. When governments reach their limits, people of faith must embrace the teachings of Jesus Christ and of the prophets of other faiths, summarized in the mandate "You shall love your neighbor as yourself." We people of religious faith have a much greater opportunity beyond government to have our hearts united, to reach out personally to those in need, and to expand our lives in demonstrating self-sacrificial love, even for the unlovable and our enemies.

There have been times when government was generally trusted to stand for some of the transcendent values that represent the best in humankind. Today, however, American attitudes toward government seem to be dominated by cynicism and pessimism. Tragically, American governments at all levels have gotten away from the concepts of forgiveness, reconciliation, and cooperation. Our society is steadily growing more racially, economically, and politically polarized. One result is that many poor and minority Americans are convinced, with good reason, that the basic system of justice and law enforcement is not fair. When the laws are shaped and administered by the most powerful leaders in a society, it is human nature for them to understand, justify, and protect the interests of themselves and people like them. Many injustices arise from this natural human failing, and we must guard against it in all areas of life.

As we seek to renew America's commitment to promote human rights and human dignity around the world, we have to be a living example here at home. As individuals, we must reject the divisive attacks based on a person's religion, race, gender, sexual orientation or identity, country of origin, or class. During one of my Bible classes in November 2017, I asked how the class would assess the current status of our nation's domestic society. The responses were instantaneous, unrestrained, and overwhelmingly negative in tone, with words like "discouraged," "divided," "aggravated," and "frustrated"— even "disgusting" and "nauseating"—prevailing. However, the reply was almost unanimously affirmative when I asked if they still had faith in our country and its ability to meet the challenges and overcome the prevailing difficulties. I recounted to them my struggling through Tolstoy's novel *War and Peace* when I was about twelve years old, and how great an impression it made on me. I told them about later making political speeches to potential supporters, saying that the primary lesson I derived from the book was that the course of even the greatest historic events was determined by the collective influence of individual citizens; and if this was true in Tolstoy's Russia governed by an emperor, how much more was it true in a democracy like ours?

The collective guidance of the American people will shape the future of our nation, but we must retain our own self-confidence, and faith in basic principles like truth, equality, justice, peace, democracy, and mutual respect even between citizens who disagree on controversial issues. This must be an active, not passive or dormant, faith. At my age, I can only hope for future national leaders who will inspire Americans with a positive vision, based on peace and human rights.

In my inaugural speech as president, I said that "I would hope that the nations of the world might say that we had built a lasting peace, based not on weapons of war but on international policies which reflect our own most precious values." I was fortunate to avoid any armed conflict while I was in office, to promote peace among other countries, and to elevate human rights to a high priority in domestic and foreign affairs. Perhaps more important, I tried to plant a lasting commitment to human rights in Latin America, China, and the Soviet Union while I was president, hoping this would pay future dividends.

Since I left the White House, the work of The Carter Center has been focused on the same general goals: peace and human rights, and we try not to deviate from these priorities. Our slogan is "Waging peace. Fighting disease. Building hope." We define human rights in their broadest sense, including all those included in the Universal Declaration of Human Rights and other related commitments. Although our Center does not espouse any religious faith, my belief is that this is what Karl Barth had in mind when he said, "Christians should support democracy, as the best State to serve people. We must seek a government and an economy that are right for the cause of Christ." I have not experienced any serious incompatibilities between my Christian faith and my responsibilities in public office or with The Carter Center.

Americans have always been justifiably proud of our country, beginning with our forefathers' bold Declaration of Independence, and our people have utilized America's great natural resources, access to warm oceans, relatively friendly neighbors, heterogeneous population, and a pioneering spirit to form a "more perfect union." Most Americans want to do what is right and fair, are concerned about others, prefer peace to war, would like to bridge the chasm between ourselves and the needy, prefer a clean and healthy environment, and profess to consider all people equal in the eyes of God.

Despite the justifiable criticism and disillusionment with political processes, it is most often governments, and not the churches, synagogues, and mosques, that have been in the forefront of the struggle to "proclaim good news to the poor. He has sent me to proclaim freedom for the prisoners and recovery of sight for the blind, to set the oppressed free," to use the words of Jesus as he announced his own ministry (Luke 4:18). What is the proper response from people of faith when there is an obvious disparity between our government's policies and our religious beliefs? The Bible is ambiguous concerning our duties in this situation. Paul told the Romans, "Let everyone be subject to the governing authorities . . . whoever rebels against the authority . . . will bring judgment on themselves" (Romans 13:1–2). With their own actions, however, Jesus, Paul, and the disciples all gave a different answer to this question, demonstrating that civil disobedience is in order when human laws are contrary to God's commands. Jesus went to his death and Paul spent his final years in prison rather than conform to religious and secular laws they could not accept. We are not required to submit quietly to the domination of secular authority without assessing whether it is contrary to our religious faith. Mahatma Gandhi, Martin Luther King, Jr., and the biblical heroes made it clear that nonviolence and tolerance are the necessary hallmarks of effective civil disobedience. Understood in this way, such action is the prerogative of any private citizen.

When I was in the White House, I disagreed with some of the existing laws I was sworn to enforce, such as those concerning energy, the environment, and abortion, and I attempted in every legitimate way to change the laws or to minimize what I considered to be their adverse effects. When governments fail to defend real justice, it is a duty for citizens motivated by their faith and a sense of morality to challenge the policies and to demand change. In the 1960s, mostly young Americans used peaceful demonstrations and sometimes more spirited forms of protest to change American policies in three of the most important issues that faced our government: civil rights, the environment, and the Vietnam War. Civil disobedience, of course, always includes a willingness to accept the penalty for violating the law one opposes. Later, in the 1980s, our daughter, Amy, was arrested on three occasions for participating in student demonstrations against apartheid in South Africa, and once she was jailed, put on trial, and ultimately found innocent for exhibiting her condemnation of the policies of the U.S. Central Intelligence Agency during the Contra war in Nicaragua. She was helped by a Massachusetts law that forgives a minor crime if it is committed to prevent a greater one.

Mostly because we enjoyed our racial advantages, many white Americans in all regions during slavery and segregation times were willing to accept these evils without questioning them, and many of our black neighbors were reluctant to challenge the racist system. Its violation of basic religious values seems clear now, but, during the era of "separate but equal" laws, it was the accepted way of life in America. When civil rights emerged in the early 1950s as a political issue, respected religious leaders were invited to speak to the members of our Plains Baptist Church. Most of our church members nodded approvingly while, with carefully selected scriptures, the speakers "proved" that separation of the races was condoned or even mandated by God. Their reassuring testimony was corroborated by members of Congress and our nation's distinguished "constitutional lawyers," including Supreme Court justices, who maintained that racial segregation was acceptable under the U.S. Constitution. I was one of those who remained largely mute and inactive.

But then a problem developed. My farm warehouse customers threatened us with a boycott because we were seen as too liberal on the issue of racial segregation. Although I didn't know which of my immediate neighbors or farm customers were members of the Ku Klux Klan, everyone knew that almost all the white men in Plains belonged to the White Citizens' Council. This was a loose organization publicly sponsored by most of Georgia's political leaders, including the incumbent U.S. senators, the governor, and other officials of the state and local governments. They collected annual dues of five dollars, issued membership cards, and had one or two public meetings each year. No one except the top leaders ever knew what happened to the dues money.

The Council members always professed to be nonracist and peaceful in their purposes, but they were decidedly against racial integration. It was understood that a line was being drawn among white citizens concerning the civil rights movement. The two Council leaders in Plains were the railroad depot agent and the town marshal, both of whom knew everyone and had time to sign up members, keep records of dues collected, and deliver pamphlets and notices. When they first called on me in my warehouse office, I told them I was not inclined to join the Council. That night I discussed the issue with Rosalynn, and we agreed that we would not yield to the community pressure, even if the decision might reduce our already marginal income from the warehouse. When the marshal came back to see me, I informed him that I did not intend to be a member. He told me I was making a serious mistake and claimed that every other white man in town had signed up.

I did not hear anything more until, one day in the early summer of 1955, about twenty of my best customers came to see me. They were respected men whom I knew well, and longtime friends of my father. The spokesman for the group said they realized that I had been in the navy for a long time, away from the South, and had worked on ships where the crews were integrated. They were sure I was not completely familiar with some of the changes that had taken place in my absence. He then quietly outlined the segregationist principles with which I was, of course, thoroughly familiar, including the supposed biblical foundation for the separation of races, potential damage to the quality of our schools if black and white students were together, and eventual destruction of the white race through the intermarriages that would inevitably occur. He reminded me about the prominent politicians who were leaders of the group and added that the Council members were equally concerned about the welfare of our black neighbors, among whom, he claimed, only a few radicals, mostly outsiders, wanted to make any change. He said that the Council was against any form of violence and that they were in no way connected with the Klan or other militant organizations.

He pointedly reminded me that all of them had traded with my father, had fond affection for our family, and knew that I was struggling with my new business after the previous disastrous year of drought. They had decided among them to pay the annual dues for me, but they needed my signature on the membership form. There was no need for me to play an active role in the organization. I believed then and believe now that most of the men had what they thought were my best interests at heart and were trying to protect me from criticism. It was a very difficult moment, and I knew that I was facing the prospect of losing a substantial portion of my trade in the surrounding community, but I decided to resolve the issue once and for all. I told the group how much I appreciated their trying to be helpful and their loyalty in continuing to be my customers. I understood their arguments and concerns, some of which also troubled me. However, I had decided not to join the White Citizens' Council and would not change my mind. It was not the payment of dues that was a problem; even with their money, I could not contribute to an organization in which I did not believe.

The leader of the group voiced his regret at my response, and they all left without any expressions of anger. For several weeks, very few customers came to trade with me. Fortunately, this was at the beginning of a dormant period in our annual business cycle, shortly after the crops were no longer being cultivated and about two months before harvesttime. During this interim, I thought a lot about leaving Plains and getting a job with some large company involved in the young but expanding nuclear power industry. In fact, I had standing offers from

General Dynamics and General Electric, the two companies with which I had been working on the building of the nuclear submarine. I did not discuss this question again with Rosalynn, though, because I really did not intend to leave home. One by one, I visited the men who had come to see me and found them to be much less concerned individually than they had seemed in the group that day. In fact, some of them resented the pressure that had been put on them to join the Council.

This was a serious crisis, but it brought Rosalynn and me even closer together. She began to help me at the warehouse, keeping the books, sending out monthly bills, and, after a year or two, settling up with a few of our customers for their entire year's trade. Our hard work and the slowly improving racial attitudes in Georgia let us survive financially. In fact, after a few months the county grand jury asked me to fill a place on the Sumter County Board of Education that my father had formerly occupied.

In Georgia, little official interference was permitted in these decisions about school integration, even from the governor's office. Following the Supreme Court's 1954 decision in *Brown v. Board of Education,* which struck down school segregation laws in all states, local boards of education, mostly comprising respected community leaders, were the focal points for decisions about racial integration of the public schools. We five (white) men and our counterparts throughout the state had to face this issue, and, although it took more than a decade, each of the two hundred local boards of education in Georgia eventually authorized school integration without violence. We avoided the public confrontations between state and federal officials that occurred in Mississippi, Arkansas, and Alabama.

Unfortunately, the overall issue was not resolved easily. For the following fifteen years (and even until today), strong segregation sentiments remained. The influence of the White Citizens' Councils slowly faded in all the Southern states except Mississippi, but in Sumter County the John Birch Society gained a stronghold. In our county seat, Americus, a majority of bankers, doctors, and lawyers were active members. The daily *Times-Recorder* newspaper always ran the John Birch column prominently on its editorial page. A number of private schools were organized by white parents who refused to permit their children to be educated with black students. Strong social and economic pressures were exerted to prevent further integration. The churches, free from government authority, were most immune to change. There was a widely published photograph of black people kneeling in prayer in front of an Americus church, confronted by a stern line of Methodist stewards with arms crossed, guarding the front door of God's house of worship.

As late as 1965, after I had been a Georgia state senator for three years, another boycott was organized against our family business. After our eldest son graduated from high school, the entire family took a three-week summer vacation to Mexico. We traveled without a specific itinerary, often staying in smaller cities, practicing our Spanish, and seeing the sights. When we returned home, I noticed that very few people came to my office as they usually did to buy feed, settle small accounts, or just visit for a while. After a few days, one of our relatives told me that he had been visited by some prominent John Birchers, who informed him where we had supposedly spent the last several weeks. I soon discovered that they had gone to the county courthouse, examined the public agricultural records, obtained a list of everyone who had ever sold peanuts to us, and then visited them all to urge that they no longer deal with our warehouse. Their story was that we had visited a Communist training camp in northern Alabama for a month, learning how to expedite racial integration in the South. These were some of the most successful leaders in our county, including the president of a large insurance agency and the man who had served in the state legislature for eight years, filling the seat my father had held. I immediately confronted these two men, who had concocted the story. Both of them claimed they had irrefutable evidence that their information was correct. It was only after I returned with hotel receipts and other records from places in Mexico that they grudgingly admitted I had not been trained by Communists. Then, as had been the case ten years earlier, I had to visit my customers one at a time in order to defuse the crisis.

Some of our friends who were racial moderates, including the president of our college, the owner of the only local radio station, and the county attorney, were forced to leave the community. We survived the boycott and other pressures because of several advantages. Although it was not often mentioned, there was a clear social benefit in belonging to one of the old pioneer families. Buried in family cemeteries near Plains are Rosalynn's and my ancestors who were born in the eighteenth century. Their many descendants were devoted members of the Baptist, Methodist, and Lutheran churches, and my father and his brother had been quite active in community affairs. My uncle was mayor of Plains for twenty-eight years, and Daddy was on the county school board and the hospital authority, and served in the state legislature. Perhaps equally important in our ability to stay was that our ties to relatives and the land were too strong to break. Ancestral lands and five generations of neighboring kinfolks were much more difficult to relinquish than a law practice, a radio station, or even the top position at the local college.

In a way, our approach to the race issue was also excused because of my mother's acknowledged "eccentricity" and because I was known to have spent a number of years in the navy. Furthermore, by the time of the boycott, Rosalynn and I were personally rooted in Plains. I was deeply immersed in our new career, and I had no doubt that I had made the right decision on leaving the U.S. Navy. Our church life provided a foundation for almost everything we did. I had been elected a deacon and was teaching the Sunday School class that my father had taught. Increasingly, the members of the churches in Plains were becoming convinced that racial discrimination was contrary to the teaching and example of Jesus.

The most notably successful merger of religion and politics was the civil rights crusade of the 1950s and 1960s. It is obvious now that the segregation and abuse of African-Americans was a gross violation of both the spirit of our Constitution and the basic teachings of Jesus. The movement led by Dr. Martin Luther King in black churches and secular organizations was watched closely by Southern segregationists, who at first judged them not likely to succeed in breaking down racial barriers. The civil rights forces merged, slowly and inexorably, always with the core of their support and their major forum in the black religious congregations. Despite setbacks, arrests, and physical abuse, leaders of the movement were inspired and strengthened by the conviction that their cause was just and that God was with them. It was a burgeoning coalition, ultimately including the politicians and the federal courts, that broke down the racial barriers of our segregated society. The adoption of peace, nonviolence, and the symbols and trappings of religion in their rallies, sermons, and songs shook the conviction of white Christians who began to doubt that segregation was compatible with biblical teachings. I saw this within my own church and community. There was an evolutionary, unpublicized conversion of many white Southerners by the civil rights leaders concerning the compatibility of their cause with the teachings of Jesus. But it was a slow process, even after President Lyndon Johnson signed the basic civil rights law in 1964, which outlawed discrimination based on race, color, religion, sex, or national origin. Seven years later it was still headline news when I declared in my inaugural speech as Georgia's governor that "the time for racial discrimination is over." Within a month I was on the cover of *Time* magazine, with a declaration that "Dixie Whistles a Different Tune."

Unfortunately, all too few religious congregations make an effective and sustained effort to break down the racial and social barriers that still divide us. One obstacle to eliminating the walls of racism is that we don't quite know what to do. How many of us white people actually know a poor black family well enough to have a cup of coffee in their living room or kitchen? Or know the names of their teenage children? Or take their kids to a movie or baseball game with our children? Or invite them to our house?

When I began running for president, I realized that no candidate from the Deep South had been elected since 1848, when Zachary Taylor was chosen to be America's twelfth president. Both the state of Georgia and I had a good record on racial issues while I was governor, and the strong advice and support of prominent African-Americans, including Andrew Young and the wife and father of Martin Luther King, Jr., made it unnecessary for me to defend my civil rights credentials.

* * *

In recent years, more than at any time in history, the United States of America has become the preeminent military power on earth, and our country has continued to increase its military budget every year. It now exceeds $700 billion annually, about equal to the total of the next nine nations combined. The next largest military budget is China's, which is one-third as large, so the only arms race is one that we are having with ourselves. Since I left office, American presidents have intervened about twenty times in foreign countries. In addition to supplying our own military forces, American manufacturers provide about one-third of the major weapons sold on the international market. It is good to know that our nation's defenses against a conventional attack are impregnable, and imperative that America remain vigilant against threats from terrorists. But as is the case with a human being, admirable characteristics of a nation are not defined by strength and physical prowess.

What are some of the other attributes of a superpower? Once again, they might very well mirror those of a person. These would include a demonstrable commitment to truth, justice, peace, freedom, human rights, generosity, and the upholding of other moral values. There is no inherent reason that our nation cannot be the international paragon of these virtues. Whenever people in any nation face a challenge or a problem, it would be good to have them look to Washington for assistance or as a sterling example.

Our government should be known, without question, as opposed to war, dedicated to the resolution of disputes by peaceful means, and, whenever possible, eager to exert our tremendous capability and influence to accomplish this goal. We should be seen as the unswerving champion of freedom and human rights, both among our own citizens and within the global community. America should be the focal point around which other nations of all kinds could marshal to combat threats to security and to enhance the quality of our common environment. We should be in the forefront of providing humane assistance to people in need, including immigrants, willing to lead other industrialized nations in sharing some of our great wealth and opportunities with those that are destitute. In achieving all these goals, our country should strive in every practical way to cooperate with other nations, many of which share these fundamental ideals. There is an unprecedented opportunity in this millennium to use our unequaled influence wisely and with a generous spirit.

There would be no real sacrifice in exemplifying these traits. Instead, our own well-being would be enhanced by restoring the trust, admiration, and friendship that our nation formerly enjoyed among other peoples. Mutual honor, trust, and respect can exist even when interests are at odds. At the same time, all Americans could be united at home in a common commitment to revive and nourish the religious faith and historic political and moral values that we have espoused and for which we have struggled during the past 240 years. Jürgen

Moltmann wrote: "The dream of freedom, equality, and happiness for all human beings—'We hold these truths to be self-evident: that all men are created equal, that they are endowed by their Creator with certain inalienable rights, that among these are life, liberty and the pursuit of happiness'—is a *human* dream. It can only be fulfilled by humanity as a whole. As long as human beings are alienated from each other by class, caste, race, and nation; as long as they live against each other and not for each other, this dream cannot be fulfilled."

As a Christian, I believe that the ultimate fate of mankind will be good. I believe that the love of God will prevail. I believe and I pray as a person of faith the words of the Lord's Prayer: "Thy kingdom come, thy will be done, on earth as it is in heaven."

AFTERWORD

This book is about faith, which is a crucial element of human life and, more specifically, of all religions. Faith, however, is not the most important commitment or consideration in our human existence or in our relationship with God or with other people. That is *love*. We must remember that "God *is* love." In the thirteenth chapter of 1 Corinthians, St. Paul makes it clear that—compared to anything else—love is preeminent. He writes, "And now these three remain: faith, hope, and love. But the greatest of these is love" (1 Corinthians 13:13). More specifically, Paul states, "And if I have a faith that can move mountains, but do not have love, I am nothing" (2 Corinthians 13:2).

Earlier, when he was asked which was the greatest of all God's commandments, Jesus replied, " 'You shall love the Lord your God with all your heart and with all your soul and with all your mind and with all your strength.' The second is this: *Love your neighbor as yourself.*' There is no commandment greater than these" (Mark 12:30–31).

ACKNOWLEDGMENTS

I am especially grateful to Dr. Walter (Buddy) Shurden, who made many valuable suggestions after examining my manuscript. He is minister-at-large at Mercer University and is my favorite Baptist theologian and historian. He is former chair of the Roberts Department of Christianity, Callaway Professor of Christianity, and executive director of the Center for Baptist Studies at Mercer. Dr. Shurden is a longtime champion of the role of freedom in the Baptist tradition, as well as other cherished convictions of traditional Baptists.

Before coming to Mercer, Dr. Shurden served as dean of the School of Theology and professor of church history at The Southern Baptist Theological Seminary, professor of religion at Carson-Newman University, and pastor of the First Baptist Church of Ruston, Louisiana.

This is my thirtieth book that has been published by Simon & Schuster, and Alice Mayhew and other editors and designers have been very helpful with their questions and suggestions.

ACKNOWLEDGMENTS

Both Dr. Steve Hochman and my wife, Rosalynn, have closely examined the text to ensure its accuracy and clarity, and my secretary, Lauren Gay, has assisted in this necessary task. I have not always taken their advice, so any remaining errors are my responsibility.

GENERAL INDEX

Abraham, 28, 50, 111
actions, faith and, 31–32, 40–41, 54,
   63–81, 97–100
Afghanistan War, 128, 136–37
African-Americans, 12, 14–15, 161, 162
   see also racism; segregation
agape, 10, 148
Ahtisaari, Martti, 139
American Convention of Human
   Rights, 25
Americus, Ga., 158
Amin, Idi, 78–79
antithesis, 53–54
anxiety, fear vs., 35–36
Ariail, Dan, 36
arms race, 41, 135, 162–63
Augustine, Saint, 61

Bacevich, Andrew, 19
Baptist Brotherhood, 97–98
Baptists, 67, 68, 101, 130
   JC as, 9, 12–13, 41, 48, 51–52, 91–92
Baptist World Alliance, 92
Baptist Young People's Union (BYPU),
   13
Barth, Karl, 2–3, 33, 45, 61, 63, 94, 151
Begin, Menachem, 50, 63, 117–18
belief, faith and, 27
Biafra, 70

Bible, 27–29, 37, 49
   see also New Testament; Old Testa-
   ment
Bill & Melinda Gates Foundation, 70
Bill of Rights, U.S., 24, 32
Bonhoeffer, Dietrich, 3, 7, 94, 125
Brezhnev, Leonid, 8
Brown v. Board of Education, 157
Brundtland, Gro, 139
Brunner, Emil, 2, 3, 63
Buber, Martin, 94
Buddhists, Buddhism, 34, 49, 50–51
Bultmann, Rudolf Karl, 3, 47, 87, 94
Bush, George W., 138

cancer, 36, 84, 118–20
Carter, Amy, 153
Carter, Billy, 79–81
Carter, Earl, 12, 71, 76, 84–85, 93, 116,
   126, 157, 160
Carter, Jack, 127
Carter, Jimmy:
   ancestors of, 159–60
   as Baptist, 9, 12–13, 41, 48, 51–52,
     91–92
   Bible study and classes of, 4, 9,
     47–49, 51, 101, 105, 115, 120, 123,
     149, 160
   cancer of, 36, 84, 118–20

INDEX

INDEX

INDEX

INDEX

INDEX

INDEX OF SCRIPTURE

ABOUT THE AUTHOR

JIMMY CARTER was born in Plains, Georgia, and served as thirty-ninth President of the United States. After this service, he and his wife, Rosalynn, founded The Carter Center, a nonprofit organization that prevents and resolves conflicts, enhances freedom and democracy, and improves health around the world. He is the author of numerous books, including *An Hour Before Daylight,* recognized as "an American classic." Since leaving the presidency in 1981, President Carter has earned a Nobel Peace Prize for his humanitarian work at The Carter Center.